"IT'S NOT ABOUT ME"

MAX LUCADO
with Len Woods

PERSONAL GUIDEBOOK

Rescue from the Life We Thought Would Make Us Happy

THOMAS NELSON
Since 1798

NASHVILLE MEXICO CITY RIO DE JANEIRO

T0053317

CONTENTS

INTRODUCTION

Some time ago Max Lucado happened upon his long-time friend Sealy Yates in a hotel lobby. They hadn't seen each other in more than a year. Sealy had a few minutes and Max had an empty stomach, so the men bought deli sandwiches, found a table, and took a seat.

Making conversation, Max casually inquired, "What has God been teaching you this year?" Sealy's answer gave Max more than a sandwich to chew on.

"What has God been teaching me this year?" Sealy reflected. "Here is what I've learned: *It's not about me.*"

The phrase stirred enough reflections inside Max's heart to become a series of messages and, eventually, a book. And because the premise of that book is so foundational and so life altering, the decision was made to put the "It's Not About Me" concept into a variety of different formats whereby it could impact the most people. The result is the guidebook before you. More than a "how-to" manual, this workbook functions as a "life priorities program." It will provide effective tools that can rescue you from the dead-end life of self-absorption our generation has wrongly assumed would bring us happiness, and it will help you discover the kind of life God intended.

HOW TO USE THIS PROGRAM

The *It's Not About Me Personal Guidebook* is designed with flexibility in mind. Notice that the table of contents highlights 14 individual "priorities." And each priority has a "Session A" and a "Session B" for a total of 28 sessions. You can work through these sessions in 28 days, 28 weeks, or however long you desire. Each session will guide you through the following sections, beginning with those for *Session A*.

Exploring: This section introduces you to the overall theme of the specific priority you are studying. If you have the opportunity to use this study in a small group setting, the questions here will serve to break the ice and warm up the group for a deeper, livelier discussion.

Reflecting: This section asks a number of thought-provoking questions about the truth just presented and about how we tend to live. The goal here is to get you to ponder the personal and eternal implications of the Bible's startling claims. We want to spark your curiosity, foster deeper understanding, and stimulate a true sense of wonder. Hopefully, your mind will be spinning—in a good sense!—as you contemplate the possibilities of embracing the "It's Not About Me" way of living.

In *Session B,* you'll discover these sections:

Reviewing: These pages reiterate the big idea of the priority, and then they take you into the life and heart of a real individual or group of people. Using conversations and interviews, case studies, and actual testimonies, these vignettes show why the truth presented in the lesson is so crucial to everyday living. Again, you'll be confronted with some questions designed to take God's truth and move it from the realm of the abstract right into your daily life.

Evaluating: In these pages, buckle up and hold on! Why? Because here the questions become a bit more personal. You'll be asked to look again or look more deeply at the scriptures Max shared, and you'll be challenged to hold up your life against the transforming truth of God.

Changing: The goal of the Christian faith isn't to get more theological information; it's that we undergo spiritual transformation. So, the goal of this section is to apply the Bible to life. We want to become "doers of the Word" (James 1:22). In these pages we ask the "Now what?" questions: "Now, in light of this truth, what do I need to *do*? How does my life need to change?"

The Guidebook is not only a map; it's a record of your hunger to want to know God better. It's a diary of your attempt to follow God more consistently.

In truth, there aren't any rules for using this Guidebook, except maybe the charge to be honest. The only limits here are your imagination. You can write out confessions, describe the deep longings of your heart, or compose a poem or song of praise to God. List any questions you have, new insights you're getting about the nature of God, the changes you'd like to see in your life, and your biggest spiritual hopes and dreams.

Try to hear and preserve what God is saying to you or, better, how Christ is *touching* you through your study. In years to come, this record of spiritual insights and divine encounter will become one of your most treasured possessions.

FINAL THOUGHTS . . .

As you begin this journey, here are a few reminders:

Pray. Before you begin, ask for God's wisdom and insight. Prior to each session, ask him to make you open to and aware of whatever he wants to show you and however he wants to change you. Ask him for the strength to persevere, especially when the enemy of our souls tries like the devil (pun intended!) to divert you and discourage you.

Take your time. This isn't a race, and it doesn't matter whether you spend 28 days, 14 weeks, or 14 months completing this study. What matters is finding a more God-honoring and satisfying life.

Listen. The Bible is known as God's *written Word*, and Jesus is called the *living Word* of God. The point? God is forever speaking! He longs for us to hear his voice, so that we might know his will and live his way. Still your soul and you will hear him.

Reflect. In our busy and distracted culture, pondering deeply is a lost art, and we are the losers for it. Biblical meditation is nothing more than letting God's truth permeate our being. Considering it, mulling it over, and deliberately allowing it to sink from our heads deeply into our hearts so that it ultimately shapes the way we live. This holy habit of reflection is indispensable to a richer spiritual life!

Find a fellow struggler. Invite someone else (or a few others) to make the journey with you—friends, neighbors, coworkers, your spouse. When the going gets tough (and it will!), you'll have each other to lean on. You will have healthy accountability to spur you on through the dry times. God does huge things in our lives when we come together with others around his Word and relying on his Spirit.

Remember the point. Think of each of these sessions as your appointment time with God. Make these priorities your own. And as you take your eyes off yourself and seek the Father, through the Son, in the power of the Spirit, you will glorify him and find true life indeed.

Glory and honor to God forever and ever.
He is the eternal King, the unseen one who never dies; he alone is God. Amen.
(1 Timothy 1:17 NLT)

PRIORITY 1:

ACCEPT
YOUR PLACE
IN THE WORLD

BUMPING LIFE
OFF
SELF-CENTER

EXPLORING

In her classic book *Mythology*, Edith Hamilton tells the timeless story of Narcissus. This legendary Greek youth was unbelievably handsome. Every girl wanted him, but he wanted no one. He left broken hearts everywhere he went. One scorned maiden finally prayed to the gods, "May he who loves not others love himself."

The goddess Nemesis heard this anguished, angry prayer and answered it. So one day, as Narcissus bent over a clear pool to get a drink, he saw his own reflection and fell head-over-heels in love—with himself!

"Now I know what others have suffered from me," he cried, "for I burn with love of my own self—and yet how can I reach that loveliness I see mirrored in the water? But I cannot leave it. Only death can set me free." And that is exactly what happened. Narcissus leaned perpetually over the pool, fixed in one continual gaze, pining away for his own image, until at last he died.

The Greeks say that when the spirit of Narcissus crossed the river that encircles the world of the dead, it leaned over the boat to catch one final glimpse of himself in the water. We get our English word and modern concept of *narcissism* from this ancient story. A narcissist is one who is preoccupied, even obsessed, with self. Handsome or not, he is egocentric. Appearance aside, she thinks life is all about her.

Truth be told, there is a stubborn streak of narcissism in all of us. Self-centeredness is the great legacy of humanity's rebellion against God (see Genesis 3). At the root of Self-Ish-Ness is—do you see it?—*sin*. And as long as we remain absorbed and consumed with our own small lives and petty desires, we will scarcely acknowledge our great Creator or be of service to our fellow creatures.

Where do you see glaring examples of narcissism in our culture (for example, bodybuilders admiring themselves in the wall-to-wall gym mirrors, and so forth)?

_____

_____

_____

_____

_____

_____

_____

Why is it so easy for us to be focused on self?

_____

_____

_____

_____

_____

_____

_____

Who is the most _unselfish_ person you know? How is that quality expressed? What impact does it have on others?

_____

_____

_____

_____

_____

_____

REFLECTING

In trying to help us bump our lives off self-center, Max reminds us of this stunning passage in Scripture:

"God raised [Christ] from death and set him on a throne in deep heaven, in charge of running the universe, everything from galaxies to governments, no name and no power exempt from his rule. And not just for the time being but forever. He is in charge of it all, has the final word on everything. At the center of all this, Christ rules the church" (Ephesians 1:20–22 THE MESSAGE).

According to the passage, what does it mean for Christ to be the focal point of the universe?

_____

_____

_____

How does this complete focus on Jesus compete with the self-centeredness of our world?

_____

_____

_____

In what situations in everyday life do you tend to become more selfish?

_____

_____

_____

Max quotes the Bible passage that says:

"But we all, with open face beholding as in a glass the glory of the Lord, are changed into the same image from glory to glory, even as by the Spirit of the Lord" (2 Corinthians 3:18 KJV).

According to this verse, how are we changed so that we are able to reflect God's glory?

_____

_____

_____

Max helps us understand our place in the world. Citing the moon as an example of how we should live, Max says:

"What does the moon do? She generates no light. Contrary to the lyrics of the song, this harvest moon cannot shine on. Apart from the sun, the moon is nothing more than a pitch-black, pockmarked rock. But properly positioned, the moon beams. Let her do what she was made to do, and a clod of dirt becomes a source of inspiration, yea, verily, romance. The moon reflects the greater light."

In what ways are we created like the moon? How should we function like the moon?

_____

_____

_____

When people look at your life, they see . . . *something*. Intentional or not, your values and actions, your choices and words will reflect something. What will that be? What message do people read in your life? The people you brush up against—the ones you live with and work with—what conclusions do they draw about you? What would they say are your priorities?

_____

_____

_____

Max quoted the Bible passage that says:

> "Beholding as in a glass the glory of the Lord, [we] are changed into the same image from glory to glory, even as by the Spirit of the Lord" (2 Corinthians 3:18 KJV).

In what ways are we changed so that we increasingly "reflect" God's glory?

_____

_____

_____

What two specific changes will you make today, so that you can move off self-center and more consistently follow Christ?

_____

_____

_____

As you conclude this first session, pray this ancient prayer written by Bonaventure, the successor to Francis of Assisi as leader of the Franciscans.

> O my God, Jesus, I am in every way unworthy of you. Yet, like Joseph of Arimathea,
> I want to offer a space for you. He offered his own tomb; I offer my heart.
>
> Enter the darkness of my heart, as your body entered the darkness of Joseph's tomb.
> And make me worthy to receive you, driving out all sin that I may be
> filled with your spiritual light.

ACCEPTING
YOUR PLACE
IN THE WORLD

REVIEWING

Life is not about you or me. That's the revolutionary "big idea" we began to wrestle with in Session A of Priority 1. We are seeing that until we "Bump Our Lives Off Self-Center" and understand how and where we fit in the big scheme of things, we will never be the people God wants, and we will never find the fulfillment we want. Let's warm up for this follow-up session by leaving the theoretical realm and dropping into the actual. Let's peek into the lives of some real people struggling with real-life, everyday issues.

Stan has been waiting all week for the big game. His favorite team just needs one victory to make the playoffs. Midway through the third quarter, with his team down by one and mounting a furious comeback, the game is preempted by a special news alert. A huge fire has engulfed an apartment building in a city about twelve miles away. Local news crews are there broadcasting live.

"Aw, c'mon!" Stan yells at the large TV screen in front of him. "We don't need live coverage—we can watch the highlights at 11:00. Aw, man, and we were just about to score! Gimme a break!"

* * * * *

"So, we're *not* going?"

"Honey, Carl worked in my division."

"Yeah, but you said you barely knew him."

"True. I barely did. He and I made chitchat on occasion. But what? I'm gonna *not* go to his funeral, and go to a Broadway musical instead? How is *that* gonna look? Everyone else will be there but me."

"Yeah, well, what about our plans? We've been looking forward to this play for three months!"

"I know, but what can I do? You act like it's my fault he died."

"I'm not saying that. I just know it'll be a long time before we get the chance to do this again."

"Look, I'm sorry. What do you want me to do?"

"I want you to put me first for once. Just once."

* * * * *

Steven is in a hurry to get to his son's soccer game. He left work a few minutes early thinking for sure he would avoid the heavy rush hour traffic. Not true. Traffic has been creeping along bumper-to-bumper for at least twenty minutes. People won't go. People won't move. Nobody will cooperate. It's a mess.

"Go, people! The light's not gonna get any greener than that! C'mon—get out of the way!" he yells at the sea of motionless bumpers in front of him.

Then, while he's glaring and fuming at all the cars, it hits him: *You know, I'm furious at all this traffic, but the truth is I'm a part of the traffic. So what am I really saying when I get this angry? That my errands and destinations are more important than everyone else's. Hmmm. Interesting. I want everyone else to just pull over and get out of my way, because deep down I really believe my plans matter more than theirs. I guess that's pretty self-centered.*

You may see yourself in these little slices of life. To which of the above scenarios do you relate the most? Why?

_____

_____

_____

In what recent situations have you put your desires ahead of another person's legitimate needs or concerns?

_____

_____

_____

_____

EVALUATING

Jesus spent his entire time in ministry bumping people's lives off self-center. Before Jesus invited his disciples to follow him, they had very predictable lives. They lived in the same place they'd been born, with family members who had been doing the same work for generations. In an instant he rocks their world.

Matthew 4:18–22 captures Jesus' amazing invitation for a Copernican shift:

> *"One day as Jesus was walking along the shore beside the Sea of Galilee, he saw two brothers—Simon, also called Peter, and Andrew—fishing with a net, for they were commercial fishermen. Jesus called out to them, 'Come, be my disciples, and I will show you how to fish for people!' And they left their nets at once and went with him.*

> *"A little farther up the shore he saw two other brothers, James and John, sitting in a boat with their father, Zebedee, mending their nets. And he called them to come, too. They immediately followed him, leaving the boat and their father behind"* (NLT).

Before you ponder the questions below, realize a few facts:

- This scene is right at the beginning of Jesus' public ministry.
- A former carpenter, Christ has just begun to preach and do miracles.
- The world has never seen or heard anyone like him.
- People are intrigued and amazed. "Could this be the long-awaited Messiah and Savior sent by God?"
- Peter, Andrew, James, and John have had some prior experience with Jesus, listening to him and observing his actions.

Got all that? Okay, now...

To what are the men being invited?

_____

_____

_____

What does the invitation require of these men? If accepted, how would this opportunity change their lives?

_____

_____

_____

Why doesn't Jesus give more details about what following him will involve?

_____

_____

_____

What word(s) do you think described how these fishermen may have felt as they responded (circle any and all that apply):

| scared | excited | anxious | relieved | confused | other: |

Would it have been possible for these men to follow Jesus while staying where they were, or without altering their lives? Can we follow Jesus, but continue to insist on following the course *we* have chosen for our own lives? Why or why not?

_____

_____

_____

"A Christian should be a striking likeness of Jesus Christ. You have read lives of Christ, beautifully and eloquently written, but the best life of Christ is his living biography, written out in the words and actions of his people. If we were what we profess to be, and what we should be, we should be pictures of Christ; [yes], such striking likenesses of him, that the world would . . . exclaim, 'He has been with Jesus; he has been taught [by] him; he is like him; he has caught the very idea of the holy Man of Nazareth, and he works it out in his life and every-day actions.' "

—Charles Spurgeon

When, if ever, did you first "meet" Jesus? What were the circumstances?

_____

_____

_____

What is the difference in saying, "Christ, I will follow your lead and live out *your* agenda" and saying, "Christ, I want you to help me accomplish *my* dreams"?

_____

_____

_____

Can you say with a clear conscience that you are following Christ right now, or are you struggling with your commitment?

_____

_____

_____

If you are not wholeheartedly living for Jesus, why the reluctance? Is there a specific area where you are going your own way?

_____

_____

What scares you about surrendering yourself completely to Jesus?

_____

_____

_____

CHANGING

Max says:

"Self-promotion. Self-preservation. Self-centeredness. It's all about me! They all told us it was, didn't they? Weren't we urged to look out for number one? Find our place in the sun? Make a name for ourselves? We thought self-celebration would make us happy. . . . But what chaos this philosophy creates."

How would this philosophy of self-promotion create chaos in a symphony orchestra? How does this philosophy create chaos in relationships and real life?

_____

_____

_____

What other life situations or relationships (such as the example of playing in an orchestra) can you think of to illustrate this point?

_____

_____

_____

HOW TO "HANDEL" GOD'S GLORY

"From beginning to end it took [Handel] 24 days [to compose the Messiah], during which time he never left his small London house. For nearly a week he left his food untouched. The servant kept muttering about how temperamental musicians could be. But then one day as he walked into the room uninvited to plead with Handel to stop and eat, he saw his master with tears running down his face and heard him saying, 'I did think I did see all heaven before me and the great God himself.' Handel had just finished writing the 'Hallelujah Chorus.' And when the king rose to his feet at the London performance, Handel's vision of God had accomplished the artist's goal: to point each one of us to the great Artist himself who helps us find our way amid the attractions and distractions that steal the glory of God and replace that vision with the sickness of our souls."

—Ravi Zacharias

On the other hand, Max wonders: "What would happen if we took our places [in the great symphony/drama of life] and played our parts?" How do you answer that?

_____

_____

"Life makes sense when we accept our place," says Max. Why does he call this "a Copernican shift"? Why is it such a big deal?

_____

_____

_____

What will it take for you to make this shift, to "discover [your] place in the universe"? What will be your first step?

_____

_____

_____

Max says:

"How do we make the shift? How can we be bumped off self-center? Attend a seminar, howl at the moon, read a Lucado book? None of these (though the author appreciates that last idea). We move from me-focus to God-focus by pondering him."

What does it mean to ponder God? What are some specific ways you can do that today?

_____

_____

_____

During the next week, look for evidence of self-centeredness in your actions and attitudes. Watch out for those situations where you typically expect to be served instead of to serve, where you are prone to take rather than to give, and where you push (even manipulate) others to meet your agenda.

A *story* for accepting your place in the world.

A young boy was trying out for a part in his school play. His mom was worried, knowing how badly he wanted a major role and fearing that he might be passed over. On the day the casting decisions were to be announced, she drove nervously to the school to pick up her son. He jumped in the car, his eyes filled with pride and excitement.

"Guess what, Mom! I got a really big part. I was chosen to clap and cheer!"

What a profound lesson for us all. Max is right. It's not about us. God is the writer and director and producer and lead actor in this great cosmic play of life. Every role is different, and everyone is important. And even when we are called upon to play what some would see as a "minor part," we can find great joy and deep fulfillment!

A two-part *exercise* for accepting your place in the world.

1. Somewhere you probably have a scrapbook or box full of old photographs. Take a few minutes to look through the box. Stroll down "memory lane." Do you find yourself skipping hurriedly over snapshots that do not include you? Why?

---

2. Jot down your thoughts about this first session about self-centeredness. What do you sense God is saying to you? What questions do you have? What changes do you feel impressed to make?

A *prayer* for accepting your place in the world.

> Give me a pure heart—that I may see thee,
> A humble heart—that I may hear thee,
> A heart of love—that I may serve thee,
> A heart of faith—that I may abide in thee.
> —Dag Hammarskjöld

PRIORITY 2::

CLARIFY YOUR
GREATEST
DESIRE

SHOW ME
YOUR
GLORY

EXPLORING

What is the most beautiful word in the English language? Countless writers and poets, editors and grammarians have offered opinions over the centuries. And some of the leading vote-getters (in no particular order) are:

- Home
- Tranquil
- Halcyon
- Lullaby
- Mist
- Laughter
- Mellifluous

- Dawn
- Hush
- Bobolink
- Luminous
- Oleander
- Willow
- Wisteria

- Chalice
- Golden
- Chimes
- Gossamer
- Melody
- Lovely

And what are some of the ugliest sounding words in English (excluding indecent words)? How about these frown-producing nominees:

- Treachery
- Gargoyle
- Cacophony
- Pessimistic
- Gritty
- Phlegmatic
- Sap

- Nag
- Jukebox
- Crunch
- Smorgasbord
- Gripe
- Plump
- Victuals
  (pronounced "vittles")

- Kumquat
- Nincompoop
- Flatulent
- Grimy
- Jazz
- Plutocrat

What other words can you add to either list?

_____

_____

_____

_____

_____

_____

_____

_____

What makes these words beautiful or ugly to our ears?

_____

_____

_____

_____

_____

_____

_____

_____

Now think about the word *glory*. How would you describe it? What kind of effect does this word produce in your mind?

_____

_____

_____

_____

_____

_____

_____

_____

REFLECTING

Max talks about God's carte blanche invitation to Moses in Exodus 33:17 (NCV), "I will do what you ask," and Moses' surprising request, not for things or actions, but for God himself.

What's your gut-level reaction to Moses' request?

_____

_____

_____

Moses prayed, "Please show me your glory" (Exodus 33:18 NCV). When—if ever—have you prayed a similar prayer? What happened?

_____

_____

_____

When have you been most blindsided by an awesome sense of the glory of God? Describe how it felt.

_____

_____

_____

If a genie offered you three wishes, what would you request? (Be honest! Resist the temptation to give a holy sounding "church answer." Say what's _really_ on your mind.)

_____

_____

_____

Now, forget make-believe genies. If God Almighty gave you permission to ask for _anything_ (and also the assurance that he would grant your desire), what would you request?

_____

_____

_____

What do our prayers reveal about us? About our truest, deepest beliefs?

_____

_____

_____

When was the last time you felt stressed, or helpless, or hopeless —and more desperate for God's presence than for his "presents"? What did you do?

_____

_____

_____

Between now and your study of Session B, pick one of the following mini-assignments to help you clarify your priorities and apply what you're learning.

- Find a beautiful place near your home (for example, a lakefront, a park, an overlook) and go there, maybe at sunrise or sunset. Spend time marveling at the glory of God revealed in his creation.

- Read Psalms 95–100 or 145–150 in a different translation or contemporary paraphrase of the Bible. You may wish to try reading from *The Message* by Eugene Peterson.

- Look for glimpses of God's glory in the people with whom you interact all day. Instead of focusing on their quirks and failures, notice instead the image of God in them.

- Get up early and spend some time just lingering in God's presence. C. S. Lewis wrote in *Mere Christianity*: "The real problem of the Christian life comes . . . the very moment you wake up each morning. All your wishes and hopes for the day rush at you like wild animals. And the first job each morning consists simply in shoving them all back; in listening to that other voice, taking that other point of view, letting that other larger, stronger, quieter life come flowing in." Push back those distractions. Be still. Listen. Ask God to show you his glory.

SEEKING THE GIVER . . . OR HIS GIFTS?
"It is a serious evil to have more regard for God's blessings than for God himself."

—John of the Cross

"The reason why we have no ease of heart or soul [is because] we are seeking our rest in trivial things which cannot satisfy, and not seeking to know God, almighty, all-wise, all-good. . . . We shall never cease wanting and longing until we possess him in fullness and joy. Then we shall have no further wants."

—Julian of Norwich

"God waits to be wanted, but he must be wanted for himself, not for some lesser good he may provide."

—Ken Boa

"God's primary agenda for our lives is not our wholeness, but his glory. He's not the divine therapist. . . . True spirituality is about far more than simply getting fixed; it is about living in such a fashion that those around us are drawn to take God more seriously."

—Dwight Edwards

CLARIFYING YOUR GREATEST DESIRE

REVIEWING

This is the concluding half of our study of Priority 2 and Max's message. Our goal here? To probe—with God's help—our hearts and to see what our deepest motivations truly are. We're trying to clarify what exactly we're after in life.

The gist of Max's message? "When our deepest desire is not the things of God, or a favor from God, but God himself, we cross a threshold. . . . You and I need what Moses needed—a glimpse of God's glory."

To help bring this essential truth down into the nitty-gritty of everyday life, you're invited to consider Warren. Warren is often called upon to pray in church. In his personal life, he prays every day without fail. Actually, if you could follow him around, you would discover that Warren engages in what could best be described as a "running conversation" with God.

What a role model! After all, we're *supposed* to focus on our Creator, aren't we? From beginning to end, the Bible stresses the importance of prayer. Prayer is an all-around good thing. And Warren is to be commended for his holy habits, right?

Before you answer, you might want to ponder Warren's words about yesterday's sermon at church:

> "Our pastor is doing a series on prayer, and he asked us to reflect on what we pray for. So, I've been doing that, and, well, what I'm seeing is not so great. In most of my prayers over the last week, I've been asking God for a bigger, newer house, to cause my stock portfolio to perform better, for a hefty end-of-year bonus, for quick results in my new diet and workout routine, for this troublesome coworker of mine to get transferred to a different office(!), for our new baby daughter to sleep through the night, and for the chance to bag at least one big buck before the end of deer season.

"It's kind of embarrassing, actually, to consider all the stuff I've been praying about. Do I look up? No question about it! Am I relying on the Lord for help? Absolutely. And yet my prayers are very, well, 'Warren-centered.'

"My focus has been less on who God is and more on what God can do. Less seeking the Giver and more about craving his gifts. Less about God's glory and more about my own comfort and success."

Is Warren unusual? Or do most people have similar habits when it comes to prayer?

_____

_____

_____

_____

God loves to answer prayers and has pledged to meet our needs. But just as life is not about us, our prayers are not ultimately about us either. What part does prayer play in your life?

_____

_____

_____

_____

In his message Max wonders:

"Why did Moses want to see God's greatness? Ask yourself a similar question. Why do you stare at sunsets and ponder the summer night sky? Why do you search for a rainbow in the mist or gaze at the Grand Canyon? Why do you allow the Pacific surf to mesmerize and Niagara to hypnotize? How do we explain our fascination with such sights?

"Beauty? Yes. But doesn't the beauty point to a beautiful Someone? Doesn't the immensity of the ocean suggest an immense Creator? Doesn't the rhythm of migrating cranes and beluga whales hint of a brilliant mind? And isn't that what we desire? A beautiful Maker? An immense Creator? A God so mighty that he can commission the birds and command the fish?

"'Show me your glory, God,' Moses begs. Forget a bank; he wants to see Fort Knox. He needs a walk in the vault of God's wealth. *Would you stun me with your strength? Numb me with your wisdom? Steal my breath with a brush of yours? A moment in the spray of the cataract of grace, a glimpse of your glory, God.* This is the prayer of Moses."

How can a person learn to pray like this? How can we get over our obsession with God's gifts and become hungrier for the Giver himself?

_____

_____

_____

Friendship comes in all kinds and levels. We have *acquaintances* (with whom we have irregular and mostly superficial conversations), *casual cohorts* (with whom we enjoy occasional, slightly deeper interaction), *companions/buddies* (with whom we regularly pal around or "do stuff" with), and *best friends* (intimate allies with whom we share a deep heart/soul/life connection).

Which of these categories comes closest to describing your own relationship with God? Why?

_____

_____

_____

What does it take to develop a true friendship with God?

_____

_____

_____

Max wraps up his talk with these words:

"Forgive my effrontery, but shouldn't Moses' request be yours? You've got problems. Look at you. Living in a dying body, walking on a decaying planet, surrounded by a self-centered society. Some saved by grace; others fueled by narcissism. Many of us by both. Cancer. War. Disease. These are no small issues. A small god? No thanks. You and I need what Moses needed—a glimpse of God's glory. Such a sighting can change you forever."

How—specifically and practically—would a glimpse of God's glory change you today?

_____

_____

_____

CHANGING

What kinds of prayers do you typically pray? Put another way, what percentage of your praying involves each of these activities? Put a percentage in front of each one.

_____ praising God for who he is (adoring him, giving him glory)
_____ thanking God for what he has done
_____ interceding for the needs/concerns of others
_____ praying for his work and will to be done on the earth
_____ admitting/confessing your own failures and sins
_____ asking God to change you
_____ requesting that God give you material things or change your circumstances

Total 100%

What steps can you take to make your prayer life become more God-honoring, more other-focused, and not so *self* centered?

_____

_____

_____

Describe a specific situation in your own life this week in which you'd like to see the glory of God displayed. What might that look like?

_____

_____

_____

A *quote* about clarifying your greatest desire.

> "The essence of prayer does not consist in asking God for something but in opening our hearts to God, in speaking with him, and living with him in perpetual communion. Prayer is continual abandonment to God. Prayer does not mean asking God for all kinds of things we want; it is rather the desire for God himself, the only Giver of Life. Prayer is not asking, but union with God. Prayer is not a painful effort to gain from God help in the varying needs of our lives. Prayer is the desire to possess God himself, the Source of all life. The true spirit of prayer does not consist in asking for blessings, but in receiving him who is the giver of all blessings, and in living a life of fellowship with him."
> —Sadhu Sundar Singh

An *exercise* for remembering that the glory of God is our mission in life, our reason for being.

Get the daily paper or a weekly news magazine. Thumb through the pages, skimming the various articles. As you do, ask these questions of each story:

- How might God get the glory in and through this situation?

- How could the people of God involved in this news story honor God in their individual situations?

- How can I pray for the righteous reputation of God to be on display in this unique circumstance?

Then get out your daily schedule. Looking at your own calendar and your scheduled activities, ask and answer the same questions:

- How might I give God glory today in and through these planned events, appointments, and meetings?

- What if these plans fall apart or go awry? How can I continue to bring honor to God?

- How can I put the righteous reputation of God on display in my unique circumstances?

A *prayer* for glorifying God.

"When Jesus had finished saying all these things, he looked up to heaven and said, 'Father, the time has come. Glorify your Son *so he can give glory back to you*. For you have given him authority over everyone in all the earth. He gives eternal life to each one you have given him. And this is the way to have eternal life—to know you, the only true God, and Jesus Christ, the one you sent to earth. *I brought glory to you here on earth by doing everything you told me to do.* And now, Father, bring me into the glory we shared before the world began.'"
(John 17:1–5 NLT, emphasis added)

What is the deepest need of our souls? The same thing Moses hungered for—a glimpse of God's glory.

PRIORITY 3:

FIND YOUR
PURPOSE
IN LIFE

DIVINE
SELF-PROMOTION

EXPLORING

Somebody somewhere once compiled a list of funny signs and witty business slogans. Here are some of the best:

- On a plumber's business card—"I repair what your husband fixed."
- At a tire shop—"Invite us to your next blowout."
- On the door of a plastic surgeon's office—"We specialize in picking noses!"
- In a smoke-free coffee shop—"If we see smoke coming out of your nose or mouth, we will assume you are on fire and take appropriate action."
- On an obstetrician's office door—"Push, Push, Push."
- At an optometrist's office—"If you don't see what you're looking for, you've come to the right place."
- On a taxidermist's window—"We really know our stuff."
- In a podiatrist's ad—"Time wounds all heels."
- On a butcher's window—"Let me meat your needs."
- In a veterinarian's waiting room—"Be back in 5 minutes. Sit! Stay!"

What's the best business sign you've seen? If you can't recall any exact slogans, what corporate logo do you think is the most creative?

_____

_____

_____

_____

If someone put a sign above your church intended to spell out, perhaps humorously, its "business," what would that sign say?

_____

_____

_____

_____

_____

_____

_____

If God had a concise slogan for his ultimate purpose, what might it be?

_____

_____

_____

_____

_____

_____

_____

What snappy saying could sum up your life (how you spend your days, what you're all about)?

_____

_____

_____

_____

_____

_____

_____

REFLECTING

Max cites a number of verses that speak of God's glory. Here are just a handful:

- *"The heavens declare the glory of God"* (Psalm 19:1 NIV).

- *Who among the gods is like you, O LORD? Who is like you—majestic in holiness, awesome in glory, working wonders?"* (Exodus 15:11 NIV).

- *By those who come near Me I must be regarded as holy; and before all the people I must be glorified"* (Leviticus 10:3 NKJV).

- *I will harden Pharaoh's heart, and he will pursue [the Israelites]. But I will gain glory for myself through Pharaoh and all his army, and the Egyptians will know that I am the LORD"* (Exodus 14:4 NIV).

> *"The Hebrew term for glory descends from a root word meaning heavy, weighty, or import-ant. God's glory, then, celebrates his significance, his uniqueness, his one-of-a-kindness."*
>
> —Max Lucado

- *Trust me in your times of trouble, and I will rescue you, and you will give me glory"* (Psalm 50:15 NLT).

- *Declare his glory among the nations, his marvelous deeds among all peoples"* (1 Chronicles 16:24 NIV).

What do you make of the Bible's tremendous emphasis on the "glory of God"?

_____

_____

_____

What exactly *is* God's glory? What does it mean to "glorify" God? How would you explain these concepts to a child? To an irreligious friend?

_____

_____

_____

A skeptic might ask: "Why is God so obsessed with *getting glory*? Is he insecure? Is he arrogant? When people demand glory and honor, we call them 'egomaniacs.' Why shouldn't we think the same of God?" How do you respond?

_____

_____

_____

In his book *Desiring God*, Pastor John Piper says:

"People stumble over the teaching that God exalts his own glory and seeks to be praised by his people [because] the Bible teaches us not to be like that. . . . How can God be for us if he is so utterly for himself?

"The answer I propose is this: Because God is unique as an all-glorious, totally self-sufficient Being, he must be for himself if he is to be for us. The rules of humility that belong to a creature cannot apply in the same way to its Creator. If God should turn away from himself as the Source of infinite joy, he would cease to be God. He would deny the infinite worth of his own glory. He would imply that there is something more valuable outside himself. He would commit idolatry.

"This would be no gain for us. For where can we go when our God has become unrighteous?"

> *"If our approach to Christian living is not unswervingly theocentric and doxological in nature, it will most assuredly degenerate into an anthropo-centric one. Or to put it more simply, God is the main point in spirituality. Yet far too often Christianity is promoted as the best way around to get God's help for making life work. What is often lost sight of is that God's primary purpose for our lives is not making them work, but making them display [his own glory] (Ephesians 2:10)."*
>
> —Dwight Edwards*

What strikes you about that explanation? Does it make sense to you? Why or why not?

_____

_____

_____

Respond to the following argument: If God is the ultimate source of life and true happiness, then he is worthy of all glory and praise. And only when we give him the glory and praise he alone deserves do we find the life and true happiness our souls crave.

_____

_____

_____

Max concludes his message by quoting these Scriptures:

> *"God made all things, and everything continues through him and for him. To him be the glory forever"* (Romans 11:36 NCV, emphasis added).

> *"There is only one God, the Father, who created everything, and we exist for him"* (1 Corinthians 8:6 NLT, emphasis added).

Then he reminds us:

"Why does the earth spin? For him.

"Why do you have talents and abilities? For him.

"Why do you have money or poverty? For him.

"Strength or struggles? For him.

"Everything exists to reveal his glory. Including you.

"To seek God's glory is to pray, 'Thicken the air with your presence; make it misty with your majesty. Part heaven's drapes, and let your nature spill forth. God, show [me] God.'"

As we conclude the first part of Priority 3, right now dare to make that prayer your own.

FINDING YOUR
PURPOSE
IN LIFE

REVIEWING

In Session A, Max reminded us of the great truth that underlies all reality and existence: *God exists to showcase God.* He unashamedly promotes himself—and why not? Perfect goodness, complete wisdom, absolute power, 100% committed to the care of his Creatures. To showcase or promote anything less (which is everything and everyone else) would be perverse and pointless! Here in Session B—the second half of Priority 3—we want to see further that part of finding our purpose in life is to understand that everything exists to reveal God's great glory. Including you and me.

To help us see why this concept is tough to grasp and even tougher to live out, here is an up-close-and-personal story.

Sharon is a rising star in the advertising universe. Oozing with personality, creativity, and energy, she has helped land some major accounts for her agency and is now overseeing two high-profile, multi-million-dollar campaigns. For her talent, Sharon is compensated handsomely. One day, she keeps telling herself, she'll pause long enough to enjoy the financial fruits of her labor.

This week has been typical. Sharon has been jetting back and forth between L.A. and New York—shooting a TV commercial for a soft drink brand on the Left Coast and overseeing photo shoots in the Big Apple for a new kids cereal. It has been quite a juggling act, with lots of snafus, but thanks to two on-the-ball assistants and a really reliable cell phone, Sharon has held it together with her trademark humor and panache. y

Until 4:00 a.m. Thursday. On a nearly empty red-eye flight west, Sharon stares at the elderly couple across the aisle. While boarding the plane in New York about midnight, they had revealed they were retired missionaries, just returning from forty years in Africa. "We're on our way to see our kids and grandkids!" they had exclaimed.

Sharon studies them—their simple dress, their quiet, sweet demeanor. The man looks a lot like her grandfather, and he's reading a Bible, just like Sharon's Pappaw used to do. The woman thumbs through some pictures of her beloved grandbabies, smiles, snuggles her head against her husband's shoulder, and closes her eyes.

Suddenly Sharon's eyes fill with tears. She tries to gather herself but finds she can't stop crying, nor can she explain why she is so overcome. Is she simply exhausted from her wild week? Is she sad—and a tad lonely—because she misses her own grandparents and family? Probably so. But lurking within her mind is another uncomfortable thought: *Look at them. They've spent their entire lives serving God and serving people in great need. And me? I'm spending my life trying to get people to buy sugary junk they really don't need!*

Deplaning at LAX, Sharon watches the couple shuffle up the jetway and into the arms of a jubilant young family. The tears come again, harder this time. But then her cell phone jars her back to reality. It's her assistant with the bad news that one of the dancers has a torn knee ligament, and won't be able to continue.

"The dancing soda bottles are the whole commercial!" Sharon snaps. "Find someone else—NOW! It's Friday morning. And I've got a 3:00 P.M. flight!"

How easy it is to lose sight of what really matters. How common for us to give our lives to insignificant causes, or to get wrapped up in trivial concerns.

One of the more recent trends in advertising is an extended sales pitch on television, made to look like a regular TV show. This approach utilizes every gimmick in the book to convince would-be buyers that they simply can't live without the product being hawked.

What is the most compelling example of this type of advertising you've seen? Have you ever purchased such a product? Did it live up to its billing?

_____

_____

_____

What do you spend your time and energy promoting? Your kids? A political party or philosophy? A business? A church? Your own reputation? Your career goals? A favorite team? Your appearance? Your financial bottom-line?

_____

_____

_____

Is it wrong to have a job like Sharon's? Does everything we say and do have to overtly mention God? How—if at all—could Sharon bring God glory in filming a commercial that featured dancing soda bottles?

_____

_____

_____

EVALUATING

In the presence of what famous person (living or dead) would you be starstruck and speechless? Why are you so awed by that person?

_____

_____

_____

Do you live in awe of God? Are you dumbstruck by his glory? Why or why not?

_____

_____

_____

Which phrase best fits how you would describe giving glory to God/praising God? Circle any and all that apply.

- serious and somber
- enjoyable and satisfying
- an act of duty
- an act of passion
- celebration
- obligation
- other (specify):

Explain your response(s).

_____

_____

_____

Max mentions how David celebrated God's glory:

> *"Bravo, GOD, bravo!*
> *Gods and all angels shout, 'Encore!'*
> *In awe before the glory,*
> *in awe before God's visible power.*
> *Stand at attention!*
> *Dress your best to honor him!*
>
> *GOD thunders across the waters,*
> *Brilliant, his voice and his face, streaming brightness—*
> *GOD, across the flood waters.*
>
> *GOD's thunder tympanic,*
> *GOD's thunder symphonic.*
>
> *GOD's thunder smashes cedars,*
> *GOD topples the northern cedars.*
>
> *The mountain ranges skip like spring colts,*
> *The high ridges jump like wild kid goats.*
>
> *GOD's thunder spits fire.*
> *GOD thunders, the wilderness quakes;*
> *He makes the desert of Kadesh shake.*
>
> *GOD's thunder sets the oak trees dancing*
> *A wild dance, whirling; the pelting rain strips their branches.*
> *We fall to our knees—we call out, 'Glory!'"*
> *(Psalm 29:1–9 THE MESSAGE).*

When was the last time you worshiped like this?

_____

_____

_____

Author Annie Dillard said that if we really understood whom it is we so blithely worship, we would wear crash helmets to church and we'd lash ourselves to the pews. What do you think she meant by this statement?

_____

_____

_____

At the end of his earthly life, Christ the Son prayed to God the Father, "I have brought you glory on earth by completing the work you gave me to do" (John 17:4 NIV).

If you're still alive and kicking, obviously God is not done with you yet. You can't say that you've completed the work God has given you to do. But are you engaged in that work? Are you living out Ephesians 2:10? It states, "For we are God's masterpiece. He has created us anew in Christ Jesus, so that we can do the good things he planned for us long ago" (NLT).

> *"In everything [God] does, his purpose is to preserve and display [his own] glory. To say his glory is uppermost in his own affections means that he puts a greater value on it than on anything else. He delights in his glory above all things."*
>
> —John Piper

What steps can you take to begin doing some of the things God might have planned for you to do?

_____

_____

_____

CHANGING

It's easy to imagine glorifying God while doing overt religious acts (for example, going to church, giving money to the poor, and so forth), but what about while doing simple, everyday acts (for example, cleaning house, driving, doing yard work, and so forth). How can we bring glory to God in mundane moments?

_____

_____

_____

Max says:

"When you think 'God's glory,' think 'preeminence.' And when you think 'preeminence,' think 'priority.' For God's glory is God's priority. God's staff meetings, if he had them, would revolve around one question: 'How can we reveal my glory today?' God's to-do list consists of one item: 'Reveal my glory.' Heaven's framed and mounted purpose statement hangs in the angels' break room just above the angel food cake. It reads: 'Declare God's glory.'"

What do we humans receive from focusing on God's glory?

_____

_____

_____

Remember, if God is the source of absolute truth and ultimate righteousness, if he really is the most glorious being in all the universe, if there is no one and nothing else like him, if he is *the* One who truly deserves ultimate honor and praise, then for him not to announce that fact would be less than truthful, would it not? For our matchless Creator to be unbothered when we ignore his infinite worth and, instead, worship unworthy things, would be illogical and bizarre. Do you agree or disagree? Why?

_____

_____

_____

Think about a scientist who found the cure for cancer and yet was silent about her discovery. Would you fault her for announcing, "Give *me* your attention! Look *my* direction"? Wouldn't such a brilliant researcher (and her great works) deserve to be publicized and promoted? Shouldn't such genius and life-giving ability be displayed for all to see? And shouldn't all others offering less effective or ineffective treatments be overshadowed by this one with the solution?

_____

_____

_____

Spend a few minutes making a case for why God *must* declare his greatness and why he *must* demand our worship.

_____

_____

_____

To hear the Scripture tell it, creation, nature, and angels all work around the clock to promote God, to advertise his greatness. What about you? What kind of "commercial" for God is your life?

A *quote* about the priority of God's glory and living every moment for his honor.

"It is not only prayer that gives God glory but work. Smiting on an anvil, sawing a beam, whitewashing a wall, driving horses, sweeping, scouring, everything gives God glory if being in his grace you do it as your duty. To go to Communion worthily gives God great glory, but a man with a dung fork in his hand, a woman with a slop pail, give him glory too. He is so great that all things give him glory if you mean they should."
—Gerard Manley Hopkins

An *exercise* for remembering that the glory of God is our purpose in life, our reason for being.

Drop by a local Christian bookstore and look at the various book titles. How many of them are human-centered (focused on our human wants or needs)? How many seem truly God-centered? What conclusions do you make of this?

A *prayer* that we make God's glory our purpose in life.

"Our Father in heaven,
may your name be honored.
May your Kingdom come soon.
May your will be done here on earth,
just as it is in heaven.
Give us our food for today,
and forgive us our sins,
just as we have forgiven those who have sinned against us.
And don't let us yield to temptation,
but deliver us from the evil one."
(Jesus speaking in Matthew 6:9–13 NLT)

PRIORITY 4:

DISCOVER YOUR
HIDDEN
STRENGTH

HOLY
DIFFERENT

EXPLORING

People have spent long hours combing the Bible in search of interesting but largely irrelevant trivia. Did you know the following fun facts?

- The longest name in the Bible, given to Isaiah's son, is Maher-Shalal-Hash-Baz (Isaiah 8:1) and means "swift is the booty, speedy is the prey".

- The shortest names in the Bible are Ai (Joshua 7:2), Ar (Numbers 21:15), Ed (Joshua 22:34), Er (Genesis 38:3), Ir (1 Chronicles 7:12), No (Jeremiah 46:25), Og (Numbers 21:33), On (Numbers 16:11), So (2 Kings 17:4), Ur (Genesis 11:28), and Uz (Genesis 10:23).

- No single verse in the Bible contains all 26 letters of the alphabet; however, Ezra 7:21 contains every letter except J.

- Only one proper name in the King James Bible begins with Q: Quartus. (Note: Other more recent translations render Cyrenius—Luke 2:2 in the KJV—as Quirinius).

- No proper names in the King James Bible begin with W or Y.

- The shortest verse in the King James Bible is John 11:35, "Jesus wept." Meanwhile, the shortest verse in the New International Version is Job 3:2, "Job said."

- The most frequently occurring word in the 1611 King James Bible is "the" (64,041 uses). The word "and" occurs 51,714 times.

- The most commonly occurring name in the Bible is "David," occurring 1,085 times. The name "Jesus" is second, found 973 times.

Isn't your heart warmed? Don't you feel closer to God already? Probably not. Those odd facts might help you on a game show someday (should "The Bible" happen to be a category), but they're *not* going to do much for your spiritual life.

What will make a huge difference in your heart and life is grappling with what the Bible says about God. In his book *The Knowledge of the Holy*, author A. W. Tozer wisely observed:

"What comes into our minds when we think about God is the most important thing about us. . . . Without doubt, the mightiest thought the mind can entertain is the thought of God, and the weightiest word in any language is its word for God. . . . A right conception of God is basic not only to systematic theology but to practical Christian living as well."

Do you agree that a person's *theology* (beliefs about God) is the most critical dimension in life? Why or why not?

_____

_____

_____

Ask around, and you'll discover that people have all sorts of different views of God. Some see him as a supernatural Santa Claus, others as a cosmic bellhop, a celestial Superman, a divine coach, or a heavenly version of their kindly, look-the-other-way grandpa. Others don't see him at all.

If you had to describe the Almighty's nature to an unbelieving friend, what words and images would you use? In other words, what is *your* view of God and what he is like?

_____

_____

_____

REFLECTING

In *It's Not About Me*, Max tells of British explorer John Speke discovering the falls of the upper Nile. What is the most awe-inspiring natural wonder you have ever seen? Try to describe how you felt.

_____

_____

_____

Max then takes us back some 750 years before Christ to the life of a Jewish prophet:

"Isaiah, face first on the temple floor. Arms crossed above his head, muffled voice crying for mercy. Like the explorers, he's just seen the unseen. But unlike the explorers, he's seen more than creation— he's seen the Creator. He's seen God."

The Old Testament book penned by Isaiah records this unexpected encounter with God using these words:

> *"Seraphim stood above Him, each having six wings: with two he covered his face, and with two he covered his feet, and with two he flew.*
>
> *And one called out to another and said,*
> *'Holy, Holy, Holy, is the LORD of hosts,*
> *The whole earth is full of His glory.'*
>
> *And the foundations of the thresholds trembled at the voice of him who called out, while the temple was filling with smoke.*
>
> *Then I said,*
> *'Woe is me, for I am ruined!*
> *Because I am a man of unclean lips,*
> *And I live among a people of unclean lips;*
> *For my eyes have seen the King, the Lord of hosts'"*
> (Isaiah 6:2–5, NRSV).

Put yourself in Isaiah's sandals. Inject yourself into this scene. Then describe what you are thinking and feeling.

_____

_____

_____

What prompted the prophet to cry, "Woe is me, for I am ruined!"?

_____

_____

_____

Max notes that Isaiah found humility "not through seeking it, but through seeking him." What does this mean? How was Isaiah changed and motivated by his encounter with God (hint: see Isaiah 6:6–8)?

_____

_____

_____

How would you explain the concept of God's holiness to a room full of fourth graders?

_____

_____

_____

What do you make of the fact that the first and final songs of the Bible (compare Exodus 15 with Revelation 15) focus on the holiness of God?

_____

_____

_____

People refer to God by using various titles or terms, for example, "Lord," "Father," even "the Man upstairs," "the big 'G'," and others. How do _you_ commonly address God?

_____

_____

_____

When in your life has God seemed the biggest? Why?

_____

_____

_____

DISCOVERING YOUR
HIDDEN
STRENGTH

REVIEWING

We're on a mind-blowing, eye-popping spiritual journey in Priority 4 of *It's Not About Me.* In Session A, we began to unlock the mystery of God's holiness. Looking at Isaiah's mysterious temple encounter with the living God, we saw that God is not merely "holy" or even "holy holy." He is "holy, holy, holy." He is so pure that sinless seraphim cannot bear to look at him!

Hopefully we are beginning to understand that those who see God most clearly regard him most highly. Hopefully we are learning that this majestic and glorious and perfect God is the One who gives our lives meaning. Not only that, but he is the One who infuses us with the power to live as we should.

Here's another real-life scene to bring these truths home into our hearts. Recently back from a short-term mission trip to northwestern Kenya, Craig is a changed man. Listen to him describe his experience:

"One day stands out. We had gone hut to hut all afternoon, telling the Turkana herdsmen and their families about Christ. They had never heard any such thing, but our translators assured us they were *very* interested. So we scheduled a showing of the *Jesus* film out in the desert later that evening. The translators told them to show up at a certain tree (which seemed crazy to me, all the trees out there look alike—especially in the dark). Honestly, I wasn't sure they'd bother to come, and I had doubts they'd even be able to locate us.

"But sure enough, about 10:00 that evening several hundred of them came streaming out the darkness. And we could tell they were excited. So we fired up our generator and used the side of our white truck as a movie screen. It was an amazing sight, sitting out there in the sand with a gentle breeze blowing, and the people were just riveted to the flickering images on the screen. They had never seen a movie before, and now they were seeing the story of

ENCOUNTERING GOD

"Is it not true that for most of us who call ourselves Christians there is no real experience? We have substituted theological ideas for an arresting encounter, . . . Whatever else it embraces, true Christian experience must always include a genuine encounter with God. Without this, religion is but a shadow, a reflection of reality, a cheap copy of an original once enjoyed by someone else of whom we have heard."

—A. W. Tozer

"I no longer want just to hear about you, beloved Lord, through messengers. I no longer want to hear doctrines about you, nor to have my emotions stirred by people speaking of you. I yearn for your presence."

—John of the Cross

God's great love and his amazing grace. Every time Jesus did a miracle—healing a sick person, casting out an evil spirit, whatever—they spontaneously clapped and cheered. The whole story was *so* real to them. They believed instantly—just like that. They wanted to know this God who came to earth to give them eternal life. I've *never* seen God's Spirit work so powerfully.

"We spent the next couple of days erecting a simple church building—sticks and mud mostly, although it did have a tin roof. When we were done, we held a worship service, a kind of dedication. I'm telling you, these people celebrated! Dancing, singing with all their might, whooping it up, feasting! You could tell it was real. I mean, it went on for hours! They were—I don't know how else to say it—*captured* by God's love. Just consumed by it. We taught them some simple Bible stories and lessons through the translators, and they hung on every word. Even the little kids. They were so hungry for the truth.

"What can I say? The trip was easily one of the top two or three experiences of my life—but it was also humbling. The truth is, I'm 39 and, I've *never* been that bowled over by Christ. Church has always just sort of been a ho-hum thing. But to see people come alive in true, heartfelt worship and total joy—even though they have almost nothing—it just gives you a whole new appreciation for who God is and what he can do. He seems so much bigger to me now. My only regret is that it took me almost forty years and a 20,000 mile trip to see it."

Have you ever been on a missions trip or had an experience in a different culture? What happened?

_____

_____

_____

What was your own salvation experience like? Was it dramatic or quiet?

_____

_____

_____

EVALUATING

Max notes a number of biblical declarations about God (some of them uttered *by* God himself). Read them again, thoughtfully:

- *Who among the gods is like you, O LORD? Who is like you—majestic in holiness, awesome in glory, working wonders?" (Exodus 15:11 NIV).*

- *For who in the skies above can compare with the LORD? Who is like the LORD among the heavenly beings?" (Psalm 89:6 NIV).*

- *To whom then will you liken God? Or what likeness will you compare to Him?" (Isaiah 40:18 NKJV).*

- *To whom will you compare me? Who is my equal?" (Isaiah 40:25 NLT).*

- *I am God—I alone! I am God, and there is no one else like me. Only I can tell you what is going to happen even before it happens. Everything I plan will come to pass, for I do whatever I wish. I will call a swift bird of prey from the east—a leader from a distant land who will come and do my bidding. I have said I would do it, and I will" (Isaiah 46:9–11 NLT).*

- *Who will not fear you, O Lord, and bring glory to your name? For you alone are holy" (Revelation 15:4 NIV).*

What theme do you see in these passages?

_____

_____

_____

What is your honest, gut reaction to these Scriptures?

_____

_____

_____

Someone has noted, "If you have a little god, you'll have big problems, but if you have a big God—the one true God—you'll have little problems." Is the God you serve and worship BIG? How awesome is he? If he's not, why not?

_____

_____

_____

How do we reconcile the biblical notion that we can be "friends of God" (Exodus 33:11; John 15:15) with stunning verses like these in 1 Timothy 6, describing who God is?

> *"[A]lmighty God, the King of kings and Lord of lords. He alone can never die, and he lives in light so brilliant that no human can approach him. No one has ever seen him, nor ever will. To him be honor and power forever. Amen" (1 Timothy 6:15–16 NLT).*

_____

_____

_____

How do the following scriptures add to your understanding of God's nature?

> *"Oh, the depth of the riches of the wisdom and knowledge of God! How unsearchable his judgments, and his paths beyond tracing out!" (Romans 11:33 NIV).*

> *"Even before a word is on my tongue, behold, O LORD, you know it altogether. . . . Your eyes saw my unformed substance; in your book were written, every one of them, the days that were formed for me, when as yet there were none of them" (Psalm 139:4, 16 ESV).*

_____

_____

_____

Because we are made in God's image (Genesis 1:26), humans have amazing creative abilities—look at humankind's great inventions and stunning works of art. What's the difference between God's creative power and ours?

_____

_____

_____

Theologians speak of God's *omniscience*. This word is from the Latin words *omni* meaning "all," and *scientia* meaning "knowledge." What does this quality of God mean to us in practical, everyday terms? What would be the implications of a Supreme Being with all knowledge but limited power?

_____

_____

_____

What's the most amazing work you've ever seen God do? The most mysterious action?

_____

_____

_____

CHANGING

Think of the most independent, secure, and powerful people on earth. In what ways are they still vulnerable? Still dependent on God?

_____

_____

_____

Omnipotence is the term Bible scholars use to speak of God's limitless power. We see this attribute on display in passages like these:

- *He is wise in heart, and mighty in strength" (Job 9:4 KJV).*

- *O Sovereign LORD! You have made the heavens and earth by your great power. Nothing is too hard for you! (Jeremiah 32:17 NLT).*

- *Praise be to the name of God for ever and ever; wisdom and power are his" (Daniel 2:20 NIV).*

- *All power is his forever and ever. Amen" (1 Peter 5:11 NLT).*

How does the truth of God's omnipotence encourage you in any current difficulties you are facing? Where do you need the Lord to show himself strong on your behalf?

_____

_____

_____

God's *omnipresence* means he is everywhere. We see this truth when King David marveled, "Where can I go from your Spirit? Where can I flee from your presence?" (Psalm 139:7 NIV). We also see it when God spoke through Jeremiah, "I am everywhere—both near and far, in heaven and on earth" (Jeremiah 23:23–24 CEV).

What is your reaction to the biblical claim that God is present everywhere? In what ways does this truth convict you today? Comfort you?

_____

_____

_____

What is the one big idea you're taking away from this lesson?

_____

_____

_____

A few *quotes* for thinking rightly about God.

"People are too apt to treat God as if he were a minor royalty."
—Sir Herbert Beerbohm Tree

"There is a God we *want* and there is a God Who *is*, and they are not the same God. The turning point in our lives comes when we stop seeking the God we want, and start seeking the God who is."
—Patrick Morley

"The final reality, and the ultimate fact of our total situation to which we need to be adjusted, is God. That indeed would be my definition of God: God is He with whom we have ultimately to do, the final reality to which we have to face up, and with whom we have, in the last resort, to reckon."
—John Baillie

An *exercise* for discovering your hidden strengths in God.

The New Testament contains several short letters written to individuals; for example, the letters from Paul to Timothy and Titus, and the "postcard" to Philemon.

Take a few minutes to imagine what God might say to *you* if you received a divinely inspired note today. Using your sanctified imagination, compose a brief epistle (500 words or less). It can be encouraging, comforting, challenging—whatever you think God wants to say to you, right where you are in life.

_____

_____

_____

A *prayer* for discovering your hidden strengths in God.

O Lord my God,
Teach my heart where and how to seek you,
where and how to find you. . . .
You are my God and you are my Lord,
and I have never seen you.
You have made me and remade me,
and you have bestowed on me
all the good things I possess,
and still I do not know you. . . .
Teach me to seek you. . . .
for I cannot seek you unless you teach me
or find you unless you show yourself to me.
Let me seek you in my desire,
let me desire you in my seeking.
Let me find you by loving you,
let me love you when I find you.
—Anselm of Canterbury

PRIORITY 5:

LIVE YOUR LIFE IN
THE LIGHT
OF ETERNITY

JUST A
MOMENT

EXPLORING

People have spent a lot of time attempting to make profound statements about time. For example:

"Time is the coin of your life. It is the only coin you have, and only you can determine
how it will be spent. Be careful lest you let other people spend it for you."
—Carl Sandburg

"Dost thou love life? Then do not squander time, for that is the stuff life is made of. . . .
Lost time is never found again."
—Benjamin Franklin

"Time has no divisions to mark its passage; there is never a thunderstorm or blare
of trumpets to announce the beginning of a new month or year. Even when a new
century begins, it is only we mortals who ring bells and fire off pistols."
—Thomas Mann

"Half our life is spent trying to find something to do with the time
we have rushed through life trying to save."
—Will Rogers

"Time flies like an arrow; . . . fruit flies like a banana."
—Groucho Marx
(A little oddball Groucho humor there, just to make sure you're still with us!)

Time. We get only so much of it—only one crack at life. So how do most of us spend this fleeting resource? The answers might surprise you. Researchers estimate the average North American living an average life span of approximately 75 years will spend:

- about 25 years *sleeping*
- about 15 years *working*
- some 10 years *watching television*
- four years *eating*
- three years *commuting/driving*
- three years *in the bathroom*
- three years *getting dressed*
- two years on the *telephone* (maybe more now that cell phones are so popular)

Are you surprised? Do you dispute any of those figures? What are some other time-consuming activities in your daily life?

_____

_____

_____

How do you decide how to spend your time? What shapes your priorities?

_____

_____

_____

If life is all about God and not about us, and if we are here solely for his glory, how should we be spending our days?

_____

_____

_____

What clues do we have in our present world regarding what the next world holds? How can eternal realities alter (for the better) our temporal, earthly experience?

_____

_____

_____

REFLECTING

In *It's Not About Me*, Max relates a story about his toddler daughter. Think back to that timeless quality of childhood in your life. What are your best and most vivid memories of those carefree days of naps and playing, with no real responsibilities and no knowledge of deadlines and time pressures?

_____

_____

_____

_____

God is eternal. Consider these verses that describe this attribute of God:

- *"God is great, and we do not know Him; Nor can the number of His years be discovered"* (Job 36:26, NKJV).

- *"You are from everlasting"* (Psalm 93:2 NKJV).

- *"From eternity I am He"* (Isaiah 43:13 NASB).

- *"The High and Lofty One Who inhabits eternity"* (Isaiah 57:15 NKJV).

- *"The living God and the everlasting King"* (Jeremiah 10:10 NASB).

- *[Jesus said],* *"Before Abraham was, I AM"* (John 8:58 NKJV).

- *"The Lord of Lords, who alone has immortality"* (1 Timothy 6:15–16 NKJV).

- *"But You [O God] are the same, and Your years will have no end"* (Psalm 102:27 NKJV).

In the space below try to put into words some of your own thoughts and feelings about the timelessness of God. What does it mean to you that God is eternal, without beginning or end.

_____

_____

_____

_____

It's been said that God is "outside of time." For him reality is not a sequence of moments ("this, *then* that, *then* that . . ."); rather, for our eternal Creator—the self-described "I AM" (Exodus 3:14)—the past, present, and future are all one big "now." Comment on this concept (if you can unscramble your brain enough to do so!).

_____

_____

_____

Consider these two passages:

- *"He has put eternity in their hearts"* (*Ecclesiastes 3:11 NKJV*).

- *"Our light affliction, which is but for a moment, is working for us a far more exceeding and eternal weight of glory"* (*2 Corinthians 4:17 NKJV*).

What does it mean that God has "put eternity" in our hearts?

_____

_____

_____

How does a conscious awareness of eternity better equip us to live out our fleeting lives here and now? In other words, in what ways does the hope of heaven give us practical help for living on earth today?

_____

_____

_____

Frederick Buechner, said: "What child, while summer is happening, bothers to think that summer will end? What child, when snow is on the ground, stops to remember that not long ago the ground was snowless?" Max writes:

"Is childhood for us what life in the Garden was like for Adam and Eve? Before the couple swallowed the line of Satan and the fruit of the tree, no one printed calendars or wore watches or needed cemeteries. They indwelt a time-free world. Minutes passed . . . unmeasured."

As we wrap up this first part of our study of "Just a Moment," are you realizing a need for a shift in your thinking . . .

. . . about God?
. . . about time and eternity?
. . . about how you use time for eternity?

Try this little mini-project—pull out your calendar or appointment book. Look over your "to do" list for yesterday or tomorrow. What jumps out at you? What do you see? What does your use of time reveal about your priorities and what you believe?

_____

_____

_____

Most important, where is God in all your plans?

_____

_____

_____

LIVING YOUR LIFE IN
THE LIGHT
OF ETERNITY

REVIEWING

If our bottom-line premise in this project is true—that is, if life is not about us—then it follows that our days and years should not be orchestrated around us. Maybe our great God has loftier reasons for putting us here. Maybe he wants us to use our time on earth for grander purposes than we imagine.

Maybe indeed.

We've been examining the mystery of time and the greater mystery of God's timelessness in the first half of this study of Priority 5. Here is a summary of what we discussed:

- Everyone has a certain number of moments. Everyone, that is, except God.

- You'll more quickly measure the salt of the ocean than measure the existence of God.

- God knows your beginning and your end, because he has neither. . . . He doesn't view history as a progression of centuries but as a single photo.

- Tucked away in each of us is a hunch that we were made for forever and a hope that the hunch is true.

- The brevity of life grants power to abide, not an excuse to bail.

- The heavy becomes light when weighed against eternity.

Those are lofty concepts and true statements, but do they work in the hustle and bustle of real life? Let's drop in on Marvin.

On the way to work this morning, Marvin had an eye-opening experience. It happened at a fast-food restaurant near his apartment. He went inside and ordered a cup of coffee. While standing at the counter, he saw a woman pull up outside at the drive-thru window and place her breakfast order. Then, whether from being shorthanded or disorganized, both Marvin and the woman had to wait about five minutes for their respective orders.

Marvin found himself getting antsy and irritated. *C'mon, people! How complicated can it be to grab that pot of coffee there, pour some into a Styrofoam cup, and hand it to me?!* He was just about to ask for his money back and walk out, when suddenly the woman outside lost it. Morphing into a kind of human volcano, she began spewing all sorts of verbal lava through the loud-speaker. Then, after getting her order, she squealed around the building to the restaurant's side door, parked, and charged inside to continue her eruption.

Marvin stood in stunned silence as this red-faced woman, veins bulging in her neck, proceeded to fuss and cuss everyone behind the counter. As the three workers sheepishly backpedaled into the recesses of the kitchen, a tired-looking middle-aged woman—obviously the manager on duty—stepped forward to try to calm the enraged customer.

No chance. No way. The Queen of Mean had a speech, and she intended to deliver it. And what a doozy it was! Concluding with a couple of choice insults and several dramatic threats, the woman whirled and was gone.

Shaking his head, Marvin looked over at the manager as if to say, "I'm sorry." Then he fixed his coffee, returned to his car, and continued on to work. The whole commute he replayed the scene in his head. *What a nightmare of a woman! Man, I'm glad she's not my wife . . . or boss! Like the whole world is supposed to revolve around her! Like her royal highness can't wait five short minutes for her precious breakfast biscuit. Yikes! How embarrassing! Imagine getting* that *worked up over something so ridiculous!*

And then it hit him. *Wait a minute—who am I kidding?* he thought. Marvin realized that he had been just as annoyed as she was. He had been ten seconds away from turning and walking out; she just beat him to the punch. Marvin wondered, *What is it about us that we get so impatient? And why do we come unglued over such minor things?*

What are your biggest pet peeves?

_____

_____

_____

Would those who know you best and love you most say you are more laid-back or more driven?

_____

_____

Are you a patient person? Do you get angry when you have to wait, or when life doesn't go your way? Why or why not?

_____

_____

_____

How do you typically react when you are angry? (put a check mark in the appropriate column)

Reaction	Never	Sometimes	Often	All the time
■ Scream/yell	❏	❏	❏	❏
■ Curse	❏	❏	❏	❏
■ Get quiet	❏	❏	❏	❏
■ Withdraw/leave	❏	❏	❏	❏
■ Throw things/slam doors	❏	❏	❏	❏
■ Pray	❏	❏	❏	❏
■ Rant/go on the attack	❏	❏	❏	❏
■ Deploy looks "that could kill"	❏	❏	❏	❏
■ Cry	❏	❏	❏	❏
■ Do the "slow burn"	❏	❏	❏	❏

Do you think it's true that maintaining an eternal perspective can make a huge difference in how we respond to the momentary trials of life—whether petty irritations or serious difficulties? Why?

_____

_____

_____

EVALUATING

We began this study thinking about the timelessness of childhood. If you could roll back the clock and relive some event or a certain day from your earliest years, what would it be, and why?

_____

_____

_____

If you could go back in time and change some decision(s) in your past, what would you do differently and why?

_____

_____

_____

Of course, we can't change the past. That is wishful thinking (and sometimes just a painful exercise). All we have is now. All we can do is make choices now. So right now, what are the frustrating situations or agonizing circumstances or faith-testing relationships that you wish you could change in a heartbeat?

_____

_____

_____

Max says:

"The brevity of life grants power to abide, not an excuse to bail. Fleeting days don't justify fleeing problems. Fleeting days strengthen us to endure problems. Will your problems pass? No guarantee they will. Will your pain cease? Perhaps. Perhaps not. But heaven gives this promise: 'our light affliction, which is but for a moment, is working for us a far more exceeding and eternal weight of glory' " (2 Corinthians 4:17 NKJV).

Is that a hard concept for you to get your mind and heart around? Do you believe it? Are you really convinced it's true?

_____

_____

_____

What resources has God provided to help us cultivate an eternal perspective?

_____

_____

_____

When in your life has heaven seemed most real and this world had its loosest grip on you?

_____

_____

_____

CHANGING

If you had a stopwatch that could freeze time (and life all around you), what would you do during such a life intermission? Read? Rest? Recreate? Catch up at the office? Finish all those home improvement projects? What?

_____

_____

_____

When it comes to time management, are you a frantic list-maker, one who is dominated by the calendar or the clock? Or are you more easygoing, just taking life as it comes, taking time to smell the flowers? Is one way better than the other? Why or why not?

_____

_____

_____

What long-term struggle are you having a difficult time enduring? What if you had to wrestle with that hardship for the rest of your life on earth—how does that prospect hit you?

_____

_____

_____

> "The heavy becomes light when weighed against eternity. If life is 'just a moment,' can't we endure any challenge for a moment? We can be sick for just a moment. We can be lonely for just a moment. We can be persecuted for just a moment. We can struggle for just a moment. Can't we?"
>
> —Max Lucado

Now, think of the promise of eternity—affliction traded for glory. How, if at all, does that divine assurance help you?

_____

_____

_____

A few *quotes* for developing an eternal perspective.

"The Present is the point at which Time touches Eternity. Of the present moment—and of it only—humans have an experience analogous to the experience which God has of reality as a whole; in it alone, freedom and actuality are offered them. He would therefore have them continually concerned either with Eternity (which means being concerned with him) or with the Present—either meditating on their eternal union with, or separation from, himself; or else obeying the present voice of conscience, bearing the present cross, receiving the present grace, giving thanks for the present pleasure."
—C. S. Lewis

"What is time? Who can easily and briefly explain this? Who can comprehend this, even in thought, so as to express it in a word? Yet what do we discuss more familiarly and knowingly in conversation than time? Surely, we understand it when we talk about it, and also understand it when we hear others talk about it. What, then, is time? If no one asks me, I know; if I want to explain it to someone who asks me, I do not know."
—St. Augustine

"Only one life t'will soon be passed. Only what's done for Christ will last."
—Anonymous

An *exercise* for remembering our eternal God and our eternal destiny.

1. Spend a few minutes thinking about the end of your life on earth. You might wish to think about your deathbed scene. Who is gathered there? What do you want to say and hear? How do you want to depart this life? (Note: This is *not* an attempt to be morbid, but an exercise in realistic thinking. Remember, we *will* each die.)

2. Think about your funeral service. How do you want to be remembered? What do you want your legacy to be?

3. Lastly, with those images and thoughts in mind, what specific changes do you need to begin making in your life *today* so that when your time on earth comes to an end, you will be able to face eternity with no regrets.

_____

_____

_____

_____

_____

_____

_____

_____

A *prayer* for living your life in light of eternity.

Lord, teach me to listen. The times are noisy and my ears are weary with the thousand raucous sounds, which continuously assault them. Give me the spirit of the boy Samuel when he said to Thee, "Speak, for thy servant heareth." Let me hear Thee speaking in my heart. Let me get used to the sound of Thy voice, that its tones may be familiar when the sounds of the earth die away and the only sound will be the music of Thy speaking voice. Amen.
—A. W. Tozer

PRIORITY 6:

CONQUER YOUR STRESS AND UNCERTAINTIES

SESSION A:

HIS
UNCHANGING
HAND

In 1967 psychiatrist Thomas Holmes developed a self-assessment tool called the "Social Readjustment Rating Scale." Educators, pastors, and counselors have used this helpful tool to measure the stressful effects of life changes that are part of the human experience.

Some of the life-change events Holmes lists include negative stress from events such as the death of a spouse, divorce, jail term, illness, losing a job, a change in residence or school. He also includes positive events that can cause stress such as marriage reconciliation, pregnancy, outstanding personal achievement, son or daughter leaving home, change in recreational activities, and vacation. Holmes' "stress test" shows without a doubt that change, no matter how big or small, is stressful and has inevitable effects on our health and well-being.

What other life events would you add to the above list? How do these things produce stress?

_____

_____

_____

Think back on your activities during the past week. What changes did you experience—large or small?

_____

_____

_____

On a scale of 1 (hardly notice the stress) to 10 (hugely stressful!), how would you rate the activities you listed in both questions above?

_____

_____

_____

_____

_____

_____

_____

How do you define "stress"? Do you think your life is stressful right now? Why or why not?

_____

_____

_____

_____

_____

_____

_____

What are some helpful and not so helpful ways that people cope with stressful times of uncertainty or change?

_____

_____

_____

_____

_____

_____

_____

REFLECTING

In *It's Not About Me*, Max tells of packing up the old family homestead and of the powerful emotions that major life event evoked. What have been the most "moving" (no pun intended) experiences in your life; that is, the biggest and most emotional changes you've had to face?

_____

_____

_____

How did you make it through?

_____

_____

_____

Max cites a number of Bible verses that refer to God's unchanging character:

- [God is] "always the same" (Psalm 102:27 NLT).

- "I the LORD do not change" (Malachi 3:6 NIV).

- [With him] "there is no variation or shadow due to change" (James 1:17 ESV).

- "
God is not a human being, and he will not lie. He is not a human, and he does not change his mind. What he says he will do, he does. What he promises, he makes come true" (Numbers 23:19 NCV).

- [He is] "the same yesterday and today and forever" (Hebrews 13:8 ESV).

- [The Lord] "will be the stability of your times" (Isaiah 33:6 NKJV).

Theologians refer to God's unchanging nature as his *immutability*. How is this quality a comfort (or how *could* it be reassuring) to someone facing uncertain times? What advantages do you see in this divine truth?

_____

_____

_____

Speaking about the inevitability of change, Max says,

"If you're looking for a place with no change, try a soda machine. With life comes change. With change come fear, insecurity, sorrow, and stress. So what do you do? Hibernate? Take no risks for fear of failing? Give no love for fear of losing? Some opt to. They hold back.

"A better idea is to look up. Set your bearings on the one and only North Star in the universe—God. For though life changes, he never does. Scripture makes pupil-popping claims about his permanence."

Why can this be a difficult concept for us to understand, to believe, and embrace?

_____

_____

_____

Compare yourself today with who you were at age thirteen. In what following ways have you changed?

Your beliefs?

Your convictions?

Your values?

Your interests?

Your hobbies?

"Created things have a beginning and an ending, but not so their Creator. The answer to the child's question, 'Who made God?' is simply that God did not need to be made, for he was always there. He exists forever; and he is always the same. He does not grow older. His life does not wax or wane. He does not mature or develop. He does not get stronger, or weaker, or wiser, as time goes by. . . . The first and fundamental difference between the Creator and his creatures is that they are mutable and their nature admits of change, whereas God is immutable and can never cease to be what he is."

—J. I. Packer

Which changes in your life were you initially convinced would be devastating but actually turned out to be good?

_____

_____

_____

In the next week become a student of people, an observer of human nature. Take a good look at the people around you. Note the changes they face and the ways they have chosen to cope with those life events.

Who do you admire? What habits or coping skills do you need to develop in your own life?

_____

_____

_____

What reactions/responses to change do you not wish to emulate?

_____

_____

_____

CONQUERING YOUR
STRESSES
AND UNCERTAINTIES

REVIEWING

Life is not about us. We're not the point. We were created by God and we were made for God and his purposes.

Those are good truths to know, but how do they help when life caves in? How do they provide comfort when we face a storm of change and uncertainty?

We're in the middle of Priority 6 and a fascinating study of God's reliable, rock-steady nature. Understanding and clinging to this truth is a sure way to begin conquering stress in times of change. In the first half of our discussion, we examined the following key points:

- Change, like taxes, is necessary but unwelcome.
- God will always be the same. No one else will.
- God's plans will never change because he makes his plans in complete knowledge.

Now, let's look into the life of Sam for a reminder of why these truths are so crucial . . .

You think *you've* got it bad? Maybe Sam's recent spate of misfortunes can give you a renewed perspective. In just the last six months, Sam has experienced:

- burying his mother (who died unexpectedly in a freak accident)
- having his eldest son "come out of the closet"
- turning 50 (and being told that despite his rigid low-fat diet and exercise regimen, his cholesterol is dangerously high)

- watching his business fail (and losing his medical insurance benefits)
- saying farewell to his two best friends (who are moving elsewhere)

In truth, Sam feels as though he has a big invisible X on his chest, and the Almighty has him in his sights and is gunning for him.

"I just feel numb, you know? It's hard to focus. It's hard to be motivated. [My wife] says I'm depressed. And maybe she's right. Am I worried? Am I bitter? Yeah, a little—no, who am I kidding? I'm worried a lot. What can I say? It's just overwhelming with so much at once. Like a series of tidal waves! You'd think God would shield me from at least a little bad news.

"I made the mistake of spilling my guts a few weeks ago during Sunday school when the leader asked for prayer requests. I must have been a little too honest because that next week I got a card and two e-mails—people bombarding me with Bible promises, and one guy chiding me for 'being negative' and 'not trusting God.'

"Well, I feel like I *am* trusting. But it isn't easy. I just want some relief. A few more bits of bad news, and I'm thinking of changing my name to Job."

If Sam were your friend, how would you try to help him deal with his stress?

_____

_____

_____

Sam mentioned some well-meaning folks who sort of "preached" at him in his distress. When did someone do this to you? What did it feel like? Is it necessary to quote a lot of Bible verses to people who are reeling and hurting? Is it wise?

_____

_____

_____

EVALUATING

How can a person develop an optimistic and positive outlook on life—especially in the face of so much uncertainty and change?

_____

_____

_____

When facing stress and change, would those who know you best and love you most describe you as:

_____ a "worrywart" (anxious and fretful)?

_____ a "kick the dog" type personality (lashing out in anger at everyone and everything)?

_____ an "Eeyore"® (Winnie the Pooh's long-faced donkey friend, always moaning, grumbling, and expecting the worst)?

_____ a "Harry Houdini" (escape artist extraordinaire)?

_____ a "Job" (not perfect, sometimes filled with doubts, but mostly marked by the resolve "Though he slay me, yet will I hope in him"—Job 13:15 NIV)?

Max comments:

"Cemeteries interrupt the finest families. Retirement finds the best employees. Age withers the strongest bodies. With life comes change. But with change comes the reassuring appreciation of heaven's permanence."

Be honest. Does heaven seem real to you? Do you long for eternity? And what would you say in response to someone who charged, "Heaven! That's just escapist thinking. Come back to the real world!"?

_____

_____

_____

Based on all you've just heard, studied, and read, what is the best thing to say to a friend like Sam, someone facing a boatload of uncertainty and change? (And, remember, it's possible to _discourage_ someone even when you're trying to be an _encouragement_! So choose your words and actions carefully.)

_____

_____

_____

What are some of the biggest changes you've experienced in just the last year:

- Relationally?
- Financially?
- Professionally/Occupationally?
- Physically?
- Emotionally?
- Spiritually?

What big societal or technological changes are you most troubled by? Most grateful for? Why?

_____

_____

_____

CHANGING

Why do you think some people fall apart at the least pressure or change in their routine, while others face huge change all the time, almost without blinking?

_____

_____

_____

On a scale of 1–10 (with 1 = "I HATE change!" and 10 = "I THRIVE on new and different!"), how would you rate _your_ overall ability to flex and adapt?

_____

_____

_____

Often it isn't the *huge* events (disaster, death, disease) that overwhelm us; rather, it is the smaller, everyday issues that combine to gradually wear us down. Rate these various types of "changes" from toughest to easiest (a "1" would be most stressful, a "10," least stressful):

_____ changing a tire
_____ changing your diet
_____ changing zip codes
_____ changing hair color
_____ changing churches
_____ changing banks
_____ changing Internet service providers
_____ changing bad habits
_____ changing retirement/investment plans
_____ changing diapers

Rank the ten most troublesome, most uncertain or "fluid" situations in your life right now from most stressful to least.

_____

_____

_____

Which is your tendency in the face of stress and change: to hold back and hide in fear or to look up in faith? Why?

_____

_____

_____

Remembering that "it's *not* about me," how can you glorify God in these unsettling, unstable situations? (Be specific!)

_____

_____

_____

What needs to change in the way you view and react to the fact of change?

_____

_____

_____

In conclusion, here's . . .

A *story* for keeping the right focus in a changing world.

A woman once remarked to E. Stanley Jones, the great missionary, "Sir, you are obsessed with the kingdom of God."

He replied, "I wish that were true. For *that* truly is a magnificent obsession."

What do people say when they look at your life? Do they see someone who is obsessed with life's problems and marked by a negative, complaining spirit in the face of change? Or do they see someone who is convinced that the unchanging God is in control and worthy of absolute trust? A person who is determined to glorify God no matter what comes?

An *exercise* for standing strong in a world filled with stress and change.

Memorize these two short verses about the *immutability* (i.e. unchanging nature) of God:

- *"I the LORD do not change"* (Malachi 3:6 NIV).

- *"Jesus Christ is the same yesterday and today and forever"* (Hebrews 13:8 ESV).

A *prayer* for conquering your stress and uncertainties.

Dear Lord,
Forgive me that so much of my religion is concerned with myself.
I want harmony with Thee. I want peace of mind.
I want health of body—and so I pray.
Forgive me, for I have made Thee the means and myself the end.
I know it will take long to wean me from this terrible self-concern, but O God,
help me, for hell can be nothing else but a life on which self is the centre.
—Leslie Weatherhead

PRIORITY 7:

CHANGE
YOUR LIFE
THROUGH LOVE

GOD'S
GREAT
LOVE

EXPLORING

Turn on the radio and you'll hear one love song after another.

You would think by now that singers and songwriters would have exhausted the subject—that there is nothing more and certainly nothing new that could possibly be said or sung about relationships. Not true. Breaking up and making up are always in vogue. And artists are forever coming up with creative ways to express their affection and their aversions.

It's worth noting that if you like your love songs served up with a splash of humor and a hint of heartache, you'll need to tune in to a country music station. That's where you'll hear songs with catchy lines like these:

- "How Can I Miss You If You Won't Go Away?"
- "I Liked You Better Before I Knew You So Well"
- "I Still Miss You Baby, but My Aim's Gettin' Better"
- "I'm So Miserable without You, It's Like Having You Here"
- "I've Got Tears in My Ears from Lying on My Back Crying My Eyes Out over You"
- "Mama Get a Hammer (There's a Fly on Papa's Head)"
- "My Wife Ran Off with My Best Friend, and I Sure Do Miss Him"
- "Please By-pass This Heart"

From these songs, what is the prevailing view of love relationships for many in our culture?

_____

_____

_____

What songs did you (or would one day like to) have sung at your wedding? Why?

_____

_____

_____

Our topic in this session, in case you didn't notice, is love. Just for fun, what's your all-time favorite . . .

- Love song?
- Romantic movie?
- Dating memory?

REFLECTING

Max cites several Bible verses, some of which may sound familiar to you:

"For God so loved the world that he gave his only Son, so that everyone who believes in him will not perish but have eternal life" (John 3:16 NLT).

"[God the Son] loved us and gave himself up for us as a fragrant offering and sacrifice to God" (Ephesians 5:2 NIV).

Do those verses excite and encourage you? If not, why not? How can we get so jaded in the face of such a staggering truth?

_____

_____

_____

According to these verses, what did God's love prompt him to do? Put another way, how has he shown his love for us?

_____

_____

_____

What does this say about our worth to God?

_____

_____

_____

_____

_____

_____

To understand a bit more of what God has done for us through Christ, think about this analogy:

You have a neighbor to whom you have been unspeakably cold and rude. You have mocked him and ignored him despite his almost daily overtures to befriend you and his regular gestures of kindness and frequent gifts. One night, a notorious serial killer breaks into your house. His intentions are clear—to make you his next victim. Suddenly your "despised" neighbor bursts into the room, apprehends the intruder, saves your life, and dies in the process.

How do you feel *now* about your neighbor?

_____

_____

_____

_____

_____

_____

How is this similar to what God has done for us?

_____

_____

_____

_____

_____

_____

A skeptical friend questions the love of God: "Look at the problems and pain of life. Look at the troubles people encounter the world over. How can you believe in a loving God in the face of such chaos and crisis?" What would you say? What evidence can you produce from your life that God is love?

_____

_____

_____

_____

_____

First John 3:1 states: "How great is the love the Father has lavished on us, that we should be called children of God! And that is what we are!" (NIV). What does it mean to "lavish" love on someone?

_____

_____

_____

_____

_____

How do we reconcile the fact that God extravagantly heaps his love on us with the rock-bottom truth that "it's not about me/us"? Don't those two concepts seem to contradict each other? Why or why not?

_____

_____

_____

_____

_____

Love comes in a variety of forms: "I love you _because_ . . ." "I'll love you _if_ . . ." "I'll love you _when_ . . ." and "I love you, _period._" How would you define the differences?

_____

_____

_____

_____

What are the drawbacks of a love that comes with conditions?

_____

_____

_____

_____

Who has given you the best example of unconditional love? Did this person's consistent care and compassion make you feel unworthy? Embarrassed? Special? Safe? Something else?

_____

_____

_____

_____

_____

As we wrap up the first part of this investigation of "God's Great Love," memorize the short verse below. Then make the commitment to meditate on it between now and the time you tackle the conclusion of this priority.

> "This is real love. It is not that we loved God, but that he loved us and sent his Son as a sacrifice to take away our sins" (1 John 4:10 NLT).

CHANGING
YOUR LIFE
THROUGH LOVE

REVIEWING

We're halfway through Priority 7, concluding a mind-boggling exploration of God's great love. In the previous session, Max explained that if life were all about us, we would shoulder an unbearable burden. Here's how Max frames it: "Do you really want the world to revolve around you? If it's all about you, then it's all up to you. Your Father rescues you from such a burden."

Thankfully, God loves us too much to leave us on our own. Is it really true? Does God love people like you and me? Max captures God's love eloquently: "Want to see the size of my love? Ascend the winding path outside Jerusalem. Follow the dots of bloody dirt until you crest the hill. Before looking up, pause and hear me whisper, 'This is how much I love you.'"

But it's not just the fact that God loves us we want to ponder. It's how this love can transform us into people who consistently reflect the glory of God.

Perhaps a true-life story can illustrate the power of undeserved, unexpected love.

John, Matt, and Luke took six inner-city boys, ages 10–12, on a church-sponsored "Wilderness Week" experience. It was an interesting seven days. Here's John's take:

> Our wilderness trip had some tense moments. Two of the kids started throwing punches at each other one afternoon while we were rock-climbing. One kid slipped on a trail, banged his knee, and let fly with a string of cuss words like I've never heard. But still, overall, it was a great trip. Most of these boys had never been outside the city limits. Never seen mountains or wildlife (except on TV, I guess). Never hiked or rappelled or camped out in a tent. And, for sure, had never experienced unconditional love. Maybe they got a little taste of that this week.

Like the night Jimmy wet his sleeping bag. The next morning the others were giving him all kinds of grief. Matt shushed them up, put an arm around this embarrassed ten year old, looked him in the eyes and said, "It's okay, bro. No big deal. Forget about it. You can have my bag tonight." You should have seen the look on that kid's face.

Another day at lunch Michael had scarfed down two hot dogs and was trying to grab a third. Luke popped his hand. The kid pleaded, "Aw, c'mon. Just one more? I'm starving!" Then he turned on the charm, "It's not my fault you make 'em so good!"

Luke smiled and shook his head. "Now, let me show you what's really good." He grabbed this skinny little guy by the arm and marched him up a steep path. Ducking to the right, they pushed through about thirty yards of thick undergrowth. Luke told me Michael's eyes almost popped out of his head as they stepped out on a rock overlooking the canyon. A small waterfall was pouring into a pool about sixty feet beneath them.

"Just listen," Luke whispered. They stood there silently for several minutes, soaking it all in—the splashing water, the shriek of a hawk in the distance, a breeze rustling the leaves overhead. Squeezing Michael's arm, Luke said, "*That's good—that's good*, my little man. Way better than a hot dog."

But the best moment was at the campfire on the last night. "Hey, why you doin' all this for us?" Devin mumbled. "You don't even know us."

Matt, a big old ex-defensive end, just looked up at Devin and grinned. "Because, bro, we want you to see that God is an awesome God. And that he loves you more than you'll ever understand."

And you know what? I think they did get a new understanding. I think they got a little glimpse. I sure pray they did.

Why do some people have a harder time believing in God's love than others?

_____

_____

_____

Whether it's the ugly duckling woman who blossoms when she is pursued and adored by a relentless suitor (think of the homely and awkward Adrian in the movie *Rocky*) or the hard-hearted Orphan Annie who is transformed by a loving adoptive family, how do you explain the life-changing power of love?

_____

_____

_____

EVALUATING

In *It's Not About Me*, Max talked about the Edwards Aquifer, an immense reservoir of water under the Texas soil. His point was that no one really knows how much water is contained there. Max likened this giant underground lake to the infinite ocean of God's love. According to the Bible it is "too wonderful to be measured" (Ephesians 3:19 CEV).

When have you felt as though your failures might somehow exhaust the limits of God's love?

_____

_____

_____

Jesus told his followers: "I have loved you even as the Father has loved me. Remain in my love" (John 15:9 NLT). What are the implications and applications of Jesus' pledge for you today?

_____

_____

_____

"So now I am giving you a new commandment: Love each other. Just as I have loved you, you should love each other" (John 13:34 NLT). How can this statement from the lips of Christ alter the way you live today? Be specific about the internal implications and the practical applications.

_____

_____

_____

When did you last feel jazzed, blown-away, overcome, or undone by God's immense love for you?

_____

_____

_____

Max observes:

"The holiness of God demanded a sinless sacrifice, and the only sinless sacrifice was God the Son. And since God's love never fails to pay the price, he did. God loves you with an unfailing love."

CHANGING

What circumstances or life situations cause you to doubt God's love?

_____

_____

_____

What does God's immense and undying love for the world, you included, tell you about his character? What does it say about your value?

_____

_____

_____

When, if ever, did God's love become more than just a word or an idea—when did it become deeply personal and real to you?

_____

_____

_____

How does knowing and experiencing God's love free us to be able to love others (especially those who are not so lovable)?

_____

_____

_____

Don't forget Max's words:

"You can no more die for your own sins than you can solve world hunger. To say 'it's not about you' is not to say you aren't loved; quite the contrary. It's because God loves you that it's not about you."

During the next week reflect on God's love for you. Listen to or sing "The Love of God," "How Deep the Father's Love for Us," and other similar hymns or songs that help you reflect on your heavenly Father's love for you.

A *quote* for changing your life through love.

"Surrender your poverty and acknowledge your nothingness to the Lord.
Whether you understand it or not, God loves you, is present in you, lives in you,
dwells in you, calls you, saves you and offers you an understanding and compassion
which are like nothing you have ever found in a book or heard in a sermon."
—Thomas Merton

An *exercise* for changing your life through love.

On a separate sheet of paper, make a list of your most spectacular failures, flaws, and foibles. Then,

- Read Ephesians 1:3–14 to get God's perspective on your miscues.
- Respond to God in prayer over the list.
- Burn, shred, or bury your list.

A *prayer* for changing your life through praise and thanksgiving for the love of God.

Praise the LORD, I tell myself;
with my whole heart, I will praise his holy name.
Praise the LORD, I tell myself,
and never forget the good things he does for me.
He forgives all my sins
and heals all my diseases.
He ransoms me from death
and surrounds me with love and tender mercies.
He fills my life with good things.
My youth is renewed like the eagle's!
The LORD gives righteousness
and justice to all who are treated unfairly.
He revealed his character to Moses
and his deeds to the people of Israel.
The LORD is merciful and gracious;
he is slow to get angry and full of unfailing love.
He will not constantly accuse us,
nor remain angry forever.
He has not punished us for all our sins,
nor does he deal with us as we deserve.
For his unfailing love toward those who fear him
is as great as the height of the heavens above the earth.

He has removed our rebellious acts
as far away from us as the east is from the west.
The LORD is like a father to his children,
tender and compassionate to those who fear him.
For he understands how weak we are;
he knows we are only dust.
Our days on earth are like grass;
like wildflowers, we bloom and die.
The wind blows, and we are gone—
as though we had never been here.
But the love of the LORD remains forever
with those who fear him.
His salvation extends to the children's children
of those who are faithful to his covenant,
of those who obey his commandments!
The LORD has made the heavens his throne;
from there he rules over everything.
Praise the LORD, you angels of his,
you mighty creatures who carry out his plans,
listening for each of his commands.
Yes, praise the LORD, you armies of angels
who serve him and do his will!
Praise the LORD, everything he has created,
everywhere in his kingdom.
As for me—I, too, will praise the LORD.
—Psalm 103 (NLT)

PRIORITY 8:

LET YOUR
LIGHT
SHINE

GOD'S
MIRRORS

EXPLORING

If you want to get a sense of what people believe, or even what causes they oppose, check out their vehicle bumpers. Schools, political candidates, life philosophies—all sorts of things get promoted on those moving plastic and fiberglass billboards we call "bumpers."

Here are some bumper stickers now showing at a parking lot near you:

- Where there's a will, I want to be in it.
- Honk if you love peace and quiet.
- If you think nobody cares, try missing a couple of payments.
- My wife, yes. My dog, maybe. My gun, NEVER!
- You're just jealous because the voices only talk to me.
- As long as there are tests, there will be prayer in public schools.
- I love animals—they're delicious!
- My karma ran over your dogma.
- Lottery: A tax on people who are bad at math.
- Forget about world peace. Visualize using your turn signal!

If you have a bumper sticker on your vehicle, what does it say?

_____

_____

_____

If you were required to promote something on your car, truck, or van bumper, what might your sticker say?

_____

_____

_____

Finally, here are two bumper stickers with more theatrical (and even theological) overtones:

- My life has a superb cast, but I can't figure out the plot.
- If all the world's a stage, where is the audience sitting?

Keeping with that drama theme, what is the best stage production/musical you've ever seen? Best movie? Why?

_____

_____

_____

Who are your favorite actors?

_____

_____

_____

If Hollywood decided to produce your life story as a Broadway play or major motion picture, who would you choose to play you?

_____

_____

_____

Have you ever acted? In school dramas? Community productions? Church skits? Were/are you typically chosen for starring roles or for smaller parts?

_____

_____

_____

REFLECTING

We were created for God or, more specifically, for God's glory. Our lives should reflect God's glory. In so many words, we should be living reflections of the greatness of God.

Max cites a passage from 2 Corinthians 3 that highlights this bedrock truth:

> "And we, with our unveiled faces reflecting like·mirrors the brightness of the Lord, all grow brighter and brighter as we are turned into the image that we reflect; this is the work of the Lord who is Spirit" (2 Corinthians 3:18 JB).

Note: The phrase "unveiled faces" is a reference to the veil Moses had to wear for some time after his face-to-face visits with God on Mount Sinai. A few verses earlier, the apostle Paul had reminded the Corinthians of this historical reality: "The people of Israel could not bear to look at Moses' face. For his face shone with the glory of God" (2 Corinthians 3:7 NLT).

Max explains two ways 2 Corinthians 3:18 can be correctly translated—"beholding as in a mirror" and "reflecting like a mirror." The former phrase conveys the idea of contemplating God's glory, while the latter idea emphasizes our need to display God's glory through our lives.

How are you doing at beholding or contemplating God's glory? Are you a reflective person, in the sense of pondering God's greatness and beauty? Where do you do this best and most effectively?

_____

_____

_____

_____

_____

_____

How are you doing at reflecting God's glory? Are you a reflective person, in the sense of shining God's greatness and beauty for others to see?

_____

_____

_____

_____

_____

Jesus encouraged his followers to "let your light shine before men, that they may see your good deeds and praise your Father in heaven" (Matthew 5:16 NIV). Think about your life over the past week—your actions, your words, your encounters with others. In what ways have you "shone"? How have you pointed people to God?

_____

_____

_____

_____

_____

_____

_____

In *It's Not About Me*, Max startles us with the image of an uncooperative mirror. His example makes us smile and shake our heads. The thought of a mirror balking at what it was created to do? *Crazy!* Unthinkable! Yet, he argues, we often do this very thing. Do you agree? If so, can you cite some personal examples where you have missed your opportunity to shine for God?

_____

_____

_____

_____

_____

_____

_____

When it comes to "promoting God," which phrase below best describes your spiritual effect on others last week?

_____ I suspect I turned people off or away from God by my self-centered, negative actions.

_____ I'm afraid I may have been a human black hole—absorbing God's blessings, but not passing them on.

_____ My life was ho-hum, with nothing especially good or bad.

_____ I think I actually may have reminded someone of the greatness of God.

_____ God's work in my life was on display—intriguing and attractive, joyful and gracious.

As you conclude the first part of this study on "God's Mirrors," realize that glorifying God doesn't mean that we make him more glorious. God is, in his very essence, already glorious—majestic, perfect, beautiful, dwelling in inapproachable light—whether we recognize it or not. As one writer put it, "Glory belongs to God as light and heat belong to the sun."

When we glorify God, we are not increasing his glory; rather, we are acknowledging his glory. We honor God and value him above all things. We make his glory known. We speak and act and think in ways that bring him positive recognition.

List five specific ways you can bring God positive recognition this week.

_____

_____

_____

_____

_____

_____

_____

_____

LETTING
YOUR LIGHT
SHINE

REVIEWING

The first session of Priority 8 is titled "God's Mirrors." In a nutshell, here's the idea we're coming to terms with.

Reduce the human job description to one phrase, and this is it: Reflect God's glory.

He's the light; we are the mirrors. The more we turn to him and focus on him, the more his character is reflected in our lives. The more we then show his character to the world, the more people shake their heads with awe, the more they marvel at our God.

That's easy to say, but not so easy to live. We struggle—some people all of the time, all people some of the time—with wanting glory for ourselves and failing to make God the focal point of life. Here's an example to ponder:

> For as long as anyone can remember, Hillside Church has sponsored an elaborate Christmas musical extravaganza. It's the big holiday event in town, complete with a huge cast, lavish sets, authentic costumes, and live animals—including this year, for the first time ever, camels!
>
> For the last five years, the lead role of Mary has been filled by one of the Crandall girls (all dark-haired and attractive, each possessing a nice singing voice). First, Karin did a two-year stint. Then Samantha took over for back-to-back years in the role. Last year sixteen-year-old Kimberly, the "baby" in the family, debuted as the mother of Jesus, following in the able foot-steps of her older sisters.
>
> Everyone has naturally assumed that Kimberly will play the Blessed Virgin again this year. But suddenly Mr. Alexander, the program director, faces an unexpected dilemma—in the person of Melissa, the sweet newcomer with the face and voice of an angel.

At the musical auditions last night, people oohed and ahhed over Melissa's amazing vocal ability. Everyone that is, except Mrs. Crandall. She sat in the back and proceeded to criticize everything about the new girl. "She's too breathy," she hissed. "And too showy!" As they were leaving, Mrs. Crandall pulled Mr. Alexander aside and reminded him how much Kimberly "has been looking forward all year" to reprising her role as Mary.

Kimberly overheard this, and she was both mortified and mystified. Back at home, her head was spinning. *Why does this matter so much to my mom? I wish she would just drop it. I already got to do the part last year. And, besides, Melissa is really good. In fact, she'd probably be the best Mary we've ever had. I don't have to be the main character. I don't even have to be in the dumb play! Wow, wouldn't that be nice? To actually just show up for once and watch. Why can't Mom see that I'm okay with not being Mary? Why can't she be okay with that? As if this whole thing is even about Mary, anyway! I thought the whole point was to focus on the baby Jesus.*

Just then, Mrs. Crandall called from downstairs, "Kimberly, come down here. I want to run through your lines with you before we head up to the church."

Kimberly buried her face in her pillow and screamed in frustration.

Why do some parents get so caught up in the activities and accomplishments of their children? What's behind this tendency to promote one's kids?

_____

_____

_____

Were your parents like this when you were growing up? Do you think previous generations were not as child-centered as today? Why or why not?

_____

_____

_____

If you are now a parent, are you this way—believing your children are to be reflections of you? Why?

_____

_____

_____

EVALUATING

Max notes a number of Bible verses that hammer home the idea that every day, and in every way, we are called to reflect God's glory.

"You are not your own; . . . honor God with your body" (1 Corinthians 6:19–20 NIV).

How does one do this—how can a person glorify God with his or her body?

_____

_____

_____

"So the sisters sent word to Jesus, 'Lord, the one you love [Lazarus] is sick.' When he heard this, Jesus said, 'This sickness will not end in death. No, it is for God's glory so that God's Son may be glorified through it' " (John 11:3–4 NIV).

Does the thought of "sickness . . . for God's glory" shock you? Why or why not?

_____

_____

_____

"Honor the LORD with your wealth" (Proverbs 3:9 NIV).

In what ways might we dishonor God in our use of money and possessions?

_____

_____

_____

Lest we assume that some areas are exempt from the job description of reflecting God's glory, we find these all-encompassing commands in the Bible:

"Whatever you do, do all to the glory of God" (1 Corinthians 10:31 NKJV).

"Whatever you do in word or deed, do all in the name of the Lord Jesus, giving thanks to God the Father through Him" (Colossians 3:17 NKJV).

Rank the following activities from 1–10, assigning "1" to the action you think might have the potential to bring God the most glory, and "10" to the action you think has the potential to bring God the least glory.

_____ singing praise songs

_____ praying silently

_____ praying publicly

_____ jogging

_____ working in a fast food restaurant

_____ preaching a sermon

_____ telling a neighbor about Christ

_____ blowing the whistle on coworkers who are stealing from the company

_____ reading your child a book

_____ resisting the urge to yell at your spouse

What's the flaw in this exercise? Do only religious actions bring God glory? Why?

_____

_____

_____

Moses had a mind-boggling encounter with the living God on Mount Sinai, resulting in Moses literally glowing with the glory of the Lord. Max writes:

> *"Paul's sewing of tents was not equal to his writing of an Epistle to the Romans, but both were true acts of worship. Certainly it is more important to lead a soul to Christ than to plant a garden, but the planting of a garden can be as holy an act as the winning of a soul."*
>
> —A. W. Tozer

"Beholding led to becoming. Becoming led to reflecting. As we behold his glory, dare we pray that we, like Moses, will reflect it?"

The sequence Max states there is extremely significant. Before we can ever reflect God's glory, we must first behold it. How much time and effort do you put into pursuing God? Do you linger in his presence? Have you developed the discipline of spending time with God?

_____

_____

_____

The great devotional writer Oswald Chambers reminds us: "We can choke God's word with a yawn; we can hinder the time that should be spent with God by remembering we have other things to do. 'I haven't time!' Of course you have time! Take time, strangle some other interests and make time to realize that the centre of power in your life is the Lord Jesus Christ and his Atonement."

What interests do you need to strangle in order to make time for reflecting on God's person and works?

_____

_____

_____

CHANGING

Let's say you are given the authority to write the script for the rest of your life, so that whatever plot you come up with for yourself, whatever role you desire to play, is yours. What does that story look like? Are you rich, famous, prominent, powerful, good-looking, what?

_____

_____

_____

Now, have you ever stopped to think of life as a great cosmic drama with God as the producer/ writer/director/and lead character? How does this thought alter the way you see your days?

_____

_____

_____

What role do you think God may be giving you to play in this great drama called life? (Hint: Look at your gifts, abilities, opportunities, experiences, passions.)

_____

_____

_____

Let's revisit and rephrase a question we asked in an earlier session: What do you mirror to others and promote—your team? your school? your business? yourself? your God?

_____

_____

_____

Are you willing to serve God wholeheartedly, and reflect his glory, even if that means you don't get the attention and acclaim others get?

_____

_____

_____

A *quote* for remembering to let your light shine.

> "I don't claim anything of the work. It is his work. I am like a little pencil in
> his hand. That is all. He does the thinking. He does the writing. The pencil has
> nothing to do with it. The pencil has only to be allowed to be used."
> —Mother Teresa

What are your thoughts of being a simple tool in the hands of God? What do you think of the notion that he can use you whenever he likes, however he chooses?

_____

_____

_____

An *exercise* for letting your light shine.

Jot down your impressions from this lesson. What do you sense God is saying to you? What questions do you have? What specific changes do you feel impressed to make?

_____

_____

_____

A *prayer* for acknowledging our failure to reflect God's glory.

Is it possible, Lord, for a soul which has received such blessings as you have bestowed on my soul, still to remain so hard and stubborn? Yes, I know it is possible, because I so frequently rebuff your advances and reject your blessings. Perhaps I am the only person alive who treats you so badly. I hope so, because I cannot bear the thought of others offending you in the same measure.

—Teresa of Avila

PRIORITY 9:

KNOW
YOUR LIFE
MESSAGE

MY MESSAGE
IS ABOUT HIM

EXPLORING

In previous generations when someone died, it was common to try to summarize a person's life or legacy on a cemetery headstone. Here are some such epitaphs (supposedly real, but some may be urban legends):

In a Ruidoso, New Mexico, cemetery:
Here lies
Johnny Yeast
Pardon me
For not rising.

In a Silver City, Nevada, cemetery:
Here lays Butch,
We planted him raw.
He was quick on the trigger,
But slow on the draw.

John Penny's epitaph in the
Wimborne, England, cemetery:
Reader if cash thou art
In want of any
Dig 4 feet deep
And thou wilt find a Penny.

In a Uniontown, Pennsylvania cemetery:
Here lies the body
of Jonathan Blake
Stepped on the gas
Instead of the brake.

In a London, England cemetery:
Here lies Ann Mann,
Who lived an old maid
But died an old Mann.
Dec. 8, 1767

A lawyer's epitaph in England:
Sir John Strange
Here lies an honest lawyer,
And that is Strange.

What epitaph would you like on your headstone, or what short funeral eulogy would you like to be made about you?

_____

_____

_____

Epitaphs may sum up our lives. But in a very real sense, our lives now are also advertising our priorities and values. What message does your life communicate to the world?

_____

_____

_____

REFLECTING

In *It's Not About Me*, Max talked about the Pony Express—the famous postal system of the Old West. He noted that the postal carriers on horseback lived bravely with one goal in view—getting letters to their recipients ASAP, AAO (against all odds).

Imagine a pony express rider who never actually delivered any mail, but rather, just spent his days "riding around" with no clear destination or purpose. What's wrong with this picture?

_____

_____

_____

Max notes two famous New Testament figures who lived not to call attention to themselves but in order to spread the message of Jesus Christ.

- John the Baptist declared, "*[Jesus] must become greater and greater, and I must become less and less*" (John 3:30 NLT).

- The apostle Paul explained: "*I have a duty to all people*" (Romans 1:14 NCV). Then he spelled out that duty. "*I am not ashamed of the gospel, because it is the power of God for the salvation of everyone who believes*" (Romans 1:16 NIV).

In contrast to these selfless souls, Max talks about his own tendency to live, at times, for the limelight and the approval of others:

"We applauseaholics have done it all: dropped names, sung loudly, dressed up to look classy, dressed down to look cool, quoted authors we've never read, spouted Greek we've never studied. For the life of me, I believe Satan trains battalions of demons to whisper one question in our ears: 'What are people thinking of you?'"

Would you regard yourself as an "applauseaholic"? Do you spend a lot of time and emotional energy obsessing over what others think of you? Explain.

_____

_____

_____

_____

_____

_____

_____

_____

Good news is for sharing; we don't have to be prodded to tell others about exciting experiences or wonderful blessings—we do it naturally. Why do you think so many Christians are tight-lipped about their faith?

_____

_____

_____

_____

_____

_____

_____

_____

Play armchair theologian/psychologist. What is behind our forgetting that we are simple messengers of good news and our frantic attempts to get attention and win acclaim from other people?

_____

_____

_____

_____

_____

_____

_____

_____

What do you talk about most? Why?

_____

_____

_____

_____

_____

_____

_____

_____

When you're out in public or at a social function, what thoughts are foremost in your mind? Check any and all that apply.

_____ "Do I look all right?"
_____ "I hope I don't say anything stupid!"
_____ Unspoken negative comments about how others look or are dressed or are acting
_____ "How can I shine for Christ in this situation?"
_____ "How can I encourage this person (or that)?"
_____ "I bet they're making snide comments about me!"
_____ Other: (specify)

Do you think more about your reputation or God's?

_____

_____

_____

_____

_____

_____

_____

_____

Over the next week observe the people around you each day (including the person who looks back at you from the mirror each morning). Look for any or all of the following:

- selfishness
- self-awareness
- self-absorption
- self-indulgence
- self-centeredness
- a self-focused attitude
- a self-serving mentality
- self-importance

KNOWING YOUR LIFE MESSAGE

The ninth of our life priorities is to know our life message. In the first part to this session, we began wrestling with the notion that we exist to convey the good news of new life in Christ. If we've experienced that eternal miracle of salvation, we will surely want to help others encounter God in a similar way. Life is not about us. It's all about him.

Let's begin with this real-life scenario . . .

In the second service on Sunday, Sheila watches the worship team and tries not to wince. It's not that they sound bad; they're actually quite talented and sound terrific. So what's Sheila's beef? In a word, Jennifer.

Jennifer is young and attractive. You could even say voluptuous. She wears very clingy dresses —sometimes (in Sheila's opinion) "dresses without enough fabric." A theater student at the local university, Jennifer is very "theatrical." Sheila is not so tactful, and says:

"She's showy. I just can't stand to watch her. It's like she goes out of her way to call attention to herself. 'Look at me. Look at how pretty I am. Look at how talented I am.' And she raises her hands and gets a little too animated. I'm sorry, but it just doesn't seem authentic. It's forced. Fake. At least it seems that way to me. Even the way she holds the microphone—it's so rehearsed, like she's seen one too many concerts. And then, those Sundays when she's not asked to sing with the worship team? She doesn't even show up at church! So is that the deal? She only comes when she gets to be up front, on center stage?

"I know I am being harsh, and probably sound really petty or jealous. I don't want to be overly critical. But it's the truth. If I look up front while we're singing, all I can see is her. And even if I close my eyes and try to think about Christ and focus on the lyrics we're singing, I've still got this image of her in my head! Because she's so loud, and I can still hear her voice above all the others."

Do you think Sheila is just envious of Jennifer? Why or why not?

_____

_____

_____

What advice would you give Sheila? How should she handle her "problem"?

_____

_____

_____

Can you relate to Sheila's dilemma? Ever faced a similar situation in which it seemed like someone (a neighbor, a family member, a coworker, a fellow church member) was always trying to grab the spotlight?

_____

_____

_____

EVALUATING

In *It's Not About Me*, Max uses the parable of a self-important guide in an art museum to illustrate how easy it is to begin to believe that we are the focal point of life. Have you ever noticed this tendency in yourself—this penchant for trying to be the center of attention? If so, when?

_____

_____

_____

Consider what the apostle Paul wrote. Using a gardening analogy to communicate the importance of helping others grow in their faith, he said: "So the one who plants is not important, and the one who waters is not important. Only God, who makes things grow, is important" (1 Corinthians 3:7 NCV).

How well do you think modern-day churches live out this truth? When have you seen Christians act "self-important"? What is the solution for this?

_____

_____

_____

Max cites Jesus—specifically, an occasion when Jesus pointed out some people of his day who were engaging in showy, "look at me!" religion:

> "When you do something for someone else, don't call attention to yourself. You've seen them in action, I'm sure—'playactors' I call them—treating prayer meeting and street corner alike as a stage, acting compassionate as long as someone is watching, playing to the crowds. They get applause, true, but that's all they get" (Matthew 6:2 THE MESSAGE).

In your opinion, how much playacting goes on among Christians? How much of what we do is intended largely to call attention to ourselves?

_____

_____

_____

If you were to take a two-week road trip with five strangers, what might they conclude about you and your deepest convictions at the end of the journey?

_____

_____

_____

A team of private investigators begins combing through your life, unbeknownst to you. What would they find? Would their report conclude that spreading the good news story of Christ is your "reason for being"? If not, what is?

_____

_____

_____

CHANGING

Max notes:

"Paul existed to deliver the message. How people remembered him was secondary. . . . How people remembered Christ was primary. Paul's message was not about himself. His message was all about Christ. . . . God doesn't need you and me to do his work. We are expedient messengers, ambassadors by his kindness, not by our cleverness. . . . Next time you need a nudge away from the spotlight, remember: *You are simply one link in a chain, an unimportant link at that.*"

How does it make you feel to realize that God doesn't *need* us to do his work; rather, he allows us to work with him—not because we are so competent, but because he is so kind?

_____

_____

_____

If other Christians in the world imitated your practices and habits of "sharing the good news of Jesus," how effectively would the message be spreading?

_____

_____

_____

A *story* for remembering that your message is about God.

A well-known youth speaker once addressed a large group of teenagers. Everything "clicked" that night. Feeding off the kids' energy and their enthusiastic response to his "off-the-wall" humor, he had the kids roaring for almost a solid hour. Driving home afterwards, he began fishing for compliments (as speakers often do) from his wife.

"That was really something, wasn't it? I can't explain it, but I was really 'on.'"

His wife said nothing for several moments. Then simply, "Yes, you were definitely hilarious, . . . too bad you didn't say anything."

A *quote* for reminding us of what matters most.

> "That which dominates our imagination and our thoughts will determine
> our life and character. Therefore it behooves us to be careful what we
> are worshiping, for what we are worshiping we are becoming."
> —Ralph Waldo Emerson

An *exercise* for remembering your place in God's plan.

God employed a number of surprising messengers in the Bible. Look up the following passages and spend a few minutes reflecting on each.

- A donkey was used to speak to Balaam (Numbers 22:21–31)
- A staff-turned-snake stirred up Pharaoh (Exodus 7:8–13)
- Stubborn oxen helped make a point about reverence (1 Samuel 6:1–12)
- A big fish was used by God to "preach a message" about obedience (Jonah 1:1–17).

What do these incidents reveal about the power of God to get his message out?

How do these examples challenge you today?

When we think of God's messengers or divine spokesmen, we tend to think of preachers and famous evangelists. But the testimony of the Bible is that God uses all kinds of people, in all walks of life to get his message across. In what specific ways do you sense God may be wanting to use you as a messenger today? To whom?

A *prayer* for strength to be his messengers.

Be assured that from the first day we heard of you, we haven't stopped praying for you, asking God to give you wise minds and spirits attuned to his will, and so acquire a thorough understanding of the ways in which God works. We pray that you'll live well for the Master, making him proud of you as you work hard in his orchard. As you learn more and more how God works, you will learn how to do your work. We pray that you'll have the strength to stick it out over the long haul—not the grim strength of gritting your teeth but the glory-strength God gives. It is strength that endures the unendurable and spills over into joy, thanking the Father who makes us strong enough to take part in everything bright and beautiful that he has for us.

—Colossians 1:9–12, THE MESSAGE

PRIORITY 10:

REFLECT
YOUR SAVIOR'S
GRACE

MY
SALVATION
IS ABOUT HIM

EXPLORING

Though humans cannot predict what *will* happen, statistics, studies, and surveys reveal much about what typically *does* happen in everyday life. In *What Are the Chances*, Bernard Siskin gives some examples:

- It is far more likely a person will die in July than in February.
- Driving in New Mexico is much riskier than driving in New Jersey.
- Farming is a much more life-threatening occupation than working as a police officer in a big city.
- The chances of a forty-five-year-old bachelor finally saying "I do" are only 1.2 percent.
- Women get bunions 3.35 times more often than men.
- Married people have better immune systems than their unmarried counterparts.
- Lower income families are 30 percent more likely to be burglarized than higher income families.
- Washing machines cause more injuries than any other cleaning equipment in the home.

Furthermore, did you know these probabilities?

- The chances of being struck by lightning are 1 in 600,000.
- The odds of winning a jackpot in the lottery are 1 in 5.2 million.
- The chance of dying in a simple fall is six times greater than dying as a result of airplane travel.
- The probability of being injured in a car wreck this year is 1 in 75.
- The chances of being killed by a poisonous snake are about the same as your odds of winning a Medal of Honor (2.6 in 10 million).

All this talk of chances and odds raises this spiritual question: What is the likelihood that imperfect, flawed people can make themselves right with a perfect, flawless Creator?

Are there things we can do to improve our "chances" for getting to heaven? How does one win God's favor?

_____

_____

_____

If you went to a nearby mall and conducted a random survey asking shoppers to rank the following people on a "goodness" scale, from BEST to WORST, what do you think the final results would be?

_____ Osama bin Laden
_____ Adolf Hitler
_____ Billy Graham
_____ Abraham Lincoln
_____ Bill Clinton
_____ Mother Teresa
_____ Apostle Paul
_____ Hugh Heffner
_____ Al Capone
_____ Mahatma Gandhi

On what basis do we usually judge someone's goodness?

_____

_____

_____

REFLECTING

Max notes:

"A large American food company released the perfect cake mix. It required no additives. No eggs, no sugar. Just mix some water with the powder, pop the pan in the oven, and presto! Prepare yourself for a treat. One problem surfaced. No one purchased the product! Puzzled, the manufacturer conducted surveys, identified the reason, and reissued the cake with a slight alteration. The instructions now called for the cook to add one egg. Sales skyrocketed."

Why are we like that? What makes people want to "add to" what is already complete?

_____

_____

_____

_____

Is it easy for you to accept gifts, or do you feel the need to do something for it? How does this human trait relate to our salvation?

_____

_____

_____

_____

Max states that the big controversy that caused so many problems in the first-century church was over circumcision. Circumcision had long been a practice of the Jews. It was intended to serve as a visible symbol of invisible spiritual realities but had degenerated into a mere external ritual. Rather than serve as a humble reminder, it became a source of pride.

By the time of Jesus and Paul, participation in this rite had become more important than a life of faith and obedience. To the legalists' way of thinking, no circumcision meant no salvation! And so Paul spoke harshly: "Watch out for those who do evil, . . . who demand to cut the body. . . . I wish the people who are bothering you would castrate themselves!" (Philippians 3:2 and Galatians 5:12 NCV).

In a nutshell, what was at stake, and why was Paul so agitated and angry when discussing this topic?

_____

_____

_____

_____

How would you define _grace_?

_____

_____

_____

_____

How would you explain *legalism* to an irreligious friend?

_____

_____

_____

Get a Bible and read about Paul's (Saul) conversion (Acts 9:1–31). What strikes you about this story?

_____

_____

_____

Reflecting on all that God had done to him, *for* him, and *in* him, Paul wrote in Romans 5:6–11:

"When we were utterly helpless, Christ came at just the right time and died for us sinners. Now, no one is likely to die for a good person, though someone might be willing to die for a person who is especially good. But God showed his great love for us by sending Christ to die for us while we were still sinners. And since we have been made right in God's sight by the blood of Christ, he will certainly save us from God's judgment. For since we were restored to friendship with God by the death of his Son while we were still his enemies, we will certainly be delivered from eternal punishment by his life. So now we can rejoice in our wonderful new relationship with God—all because of what our Lord Jesus Christ has done for us in making us friends of God" (NLT).

To whom does Paul give the credit for his salvation in this passage?

_____

_____

_____

Max says that people who think they can do something to earn or deserve salvation do not have a realistic understanding of the severity of their sin problem, as these verses indicate:

"There is no one who always does what is right, not even one" (Romans 3:10 NCV).

"For my own sake and for the honor of my name I will hold back my anger and not wipe you out. I refined you in the furnace of affliction, but found no silver there. You are worthless, with nothing good in you at all. Yet for my own sake—yes, for my own sake—I will save you from my anger and not destroy you lest the heathen say their gods have conquered me. I will not let them have my glory" (Isaiah 48:9–11 TLB).

Do you agree that we will never appreciate God's grace until we first come to grips with our utter lostness before God? Why or why not?

_____

_____

_____

_____

_____

_____

Spend some time reflecting on these matters. In preparation for Session B, do the following:

- Consider the acrostic G.O.S.P.E.L. (God Offers Sinful People Eternal Life). Why is this a good summary of the purpose for Jesus' coming to earth and what he will do for those who put their trust in him?

_____

_____

_____

_____

_____

_____

■ British author C. S. Lewis observed that we humans are not decent people who need to clean up our lives a little bit, but we are rebels who need to lay down our arms. If so, how does this grim realization that we are God's enemies (see Romans 5:10) pave the way for experiencing God's grace?

_____

_____

_____

_____

_____

_____

REFLECTING
YOUR SAVIOR'S
GRACE

REVIEWING

So far in this discussion of Priority 10, we have seen that we are selfish people. Our lives are marked by self-absorption and self-interest. Because of self-deception, we minimize our faults and exaggerate our strengths. Then, foolishly, when we have problems, we generally rely on self-help.

The problem with such a self-centered approach is that our greatest dilemma—separation from God—can never be solved by looking within ourselves. Selfishness cannot save us; it is, in fact, the very thing that is killing us!

In this session we will contemplate the miracle and mystery of God's *grace*—and our human tendency toward *legalism* (or religious self-help).

Max describes legalism with these words:

- A theology of "Jesus +"
- "Self-salvation [which] makes light of our problem"
- The attempt "to earn heaven"
- As "joyless, because . . . there is always another class to attend, person to teach, mouth to feed"

Not only are legalism's attempts to earn God's approval futile, but the entire focus is backwards. When it comes to our "eternal rescue," the hero is Jesus, not us. It's all about him. Our role is simply to receive God's amazing grace.

To begin part two of this study, let's drop in on two neighbors in a bleak neighborhood on the wrong side of town:

Shauna is a single mom who works two jobs to provide for her three young boys. She's trying hard to do right. She takes her family to church every chance she gets. She tithes on her meager income. She prays all the time. As she's leaving for worship services on this gray Sunday morning, her words reveal her disgust as well as her dreams of somehow escaping her surroundings, and her unsavory neighbors.

"Look around. Just look at this place. Drug dealers, prostitutes, gang bangers—all up and down the street. How am I supposed to raise children in this mess? See my neighbor across the way? Yeah, there she is, right there, looking out the window. Probably waiting for her next boyfriend. That's Erika. She's got a parade of men coming through there every day. And it ain't like she don't know better. You know who her daddy was? Reverend Johnson of Mt. Zion Church. Can you believe that? A fine man of God, and a daughter like that! That girl's momma, rest her soul, was the kindest and wisest woman I ever knew in my life. And now Erika wants to go off and live like a fool. Well, I'm not gonna lie—I can't even stand to look at her. And I sure don't want my boys seeing all that."

Across the street, Erika watches Shauna load up her boys in a beat-up Pontiac Firebird. She thinks back to her own childhood—Sunday morning memories of robust singing, Bible stories, fiery sermons, and big pitch-in dinners. She remembers the day of her baptism and the new white dress she wore for the occasion. How good she felt! How proud she was to be the preacher's daughter, and God's daughter too.

She closes the blinds, slumps on the couch and uses her bathrobe sleeve to wipe at the tears that have begun to fall. Lying there shaking and sobbing, she wonders, *How did I get in this place? How did I make such a mess of my life? God, I'd give anything to be able to turn back the clock. There's so much I wish I could undo—so many terrible things. But I'll never be able to return to church. Forgiveness? Not for me. Mercy? Compassion? Ha! They'd all treat me just like Shauna does. They'd make me feel even more guilty than I already feel.*

Can you understand Shauna's concerns? What stopped her from showing grace?

_____

_____

_____

What do you make of Erika's thoughts? Can you relate to her feelings of unworthiness? What stopped her from accepting grace?

_____

_____

_____

Among those who are irreligious or unchurched, do you think Christians and churches are viewed as more gracious or more legalistic? Why?

_____

_____

_____

EVALUATING

Grace means "unmerited favor." It means that we get what we don't deserve; that we receive something we didn't work for and couldn't possibly earn. We see God's grace spelled out in passages like these:

> "God's way of making us right with himself depends on faith—counting on Christ alone" (Philippians 3:9 TLB, emphasis added).

> "God saved you by his special favor when you believed. And you can't take credit for this; it is a gift from God. Salvation is not a reward for the good things we have done, so none of us can boast about it" (Ephesians 2:8–9 NLT).

> "But those who depend on the law to make them right with God are under his curse, for the Scriptures say, 'Cursed is everyone who does not observe and obey all these commands that are written in God's Book of the Law.' Consequently, it is clear that no one can ever be right with God by trying to keep the law. For the Scriptures say, 'It is through faith that a righteous person has life'" (Galatians 3:10–11 NLT).

According to the Bible, how are we made right with God?

_____

_____

"Can you add anything to this salvation? No. The work is finished. Can you earn this salvation? No. Don't dishonor God by trying. Dare we boast about this salvation? By no means. The giver of bread, not the beggar, deserves praise. 'Let him who boasts boast in the Lord' (1 Corinthians 1:31). It's not about what we do; it's all about what he does."

—Max Lucado

Is it difficult for you to accept the news that salvation is a free gift—that you cannot earn it? Why or why not?

_____

_____

_____

Someone has observed that religion is spelled "D-O." That is, it's all the stuff we think we have to *do* to win God's approval and his forgiveness. But the Christian gospel is spelled "D-O-N-E." In other words, it gives us the marvelous news that *Christ has done everything* necessary to bring us into a right relationship with God. All we have to do is trust in him and receive his free gift. The best part of the good news is not that we are lovable, but that God is marvelous and gracious. The main point is not that we have such great value but that we have such an amazing Savior.

Is this your understanding of the message of Christ?

_____

_____

_____

Legalism is that prideful tendency to add to the gospel. We want to contribute something to our salvation. Which of the following "religious formulas" are you tempted to buy into?

- Jesus + evangelism: How many people have you led to Christ this year?
- Jesus + contribution: Are you giving all you can to the church?
- Jesus + mysticism: You do spend hours in meditation, don't you?
- Jesus + heritage: Were you raised in "the church"?
- Jesus + doctrine: When you were baptized, was the water running or still? Deep or shallow? Hot or cold?

If we can't earn salvation in any of these ways, and if we can't even chip in a little bit, do we have any reason at all to boast about our right standing with God?

_____

_____

_____

_____

CHANGING

What do you sense God saying to you in this study about battling your selfishness and pride, and working for your salvation?

_____

_____

_____

How does your understanding of the message of Christ need to change?

_____

_____

_____

Who in your sphere of influence most needs to hear about Christ's unconditional love and acceptance?

_____

_____

_____

A *quote* for reflecting your Savior's grace.

"I want to simplify your lives. When others are telling you to read more, I want to tell you to read less; when others are telling you to do more, I want to tell you to do less. The world does not need more of you; it needs more of God. Your friends do not need more of you; they need more of God. And you don't need more of you; you need more of God."
—Eugene Peterson

A *"mini-Bible study"* for remembering that salvation is all about God.

"Then Jesus told this story to some who had great self-confidence and scorned everyone else: 'Two men went to the Temple to pray. One was a Pharisee, and the other was a dishonest tax collector. The proud Pharisee stood by himself and prayed this prayer: "I thank you, God, that I am not a sinner like everyone else, especially like that tax collector over there! For I never cheat, I don't sin, I don't commit adultery, I fast twice a week, and I give you a tenth of my income." But the tax collector stood at a distance and dared not even lift his eyes to heaven as he prayed. Instead, *he beat his chest in sorrow, saying, "O God, be merciful to me, for I am a sinner." I tell you, this sinner, not the Pharisee, returned home justified before God. For the proud will be humbled, but the humble will be honored.'"*

—Luke 18:9–14 (NLT)

What is the main lesson that Jesus is teaching here?

_____

_____

_____

A *prayer* for reflecting your Savior's grace.

Lord Jesus, we are silly sheep who have dared to stand before you and
try to bribe you with our preposterous portfolios. Suddenly we have come to
our senses. We are sorry and ask you to forgive us. Give us the grace to admit we are
ragamuffins, to embrace our brokenness, to celebrate your mercy when we are at
our weakest, to rely on your mercy no matter what we may do.

Dear Jesus, gift us to stop grandstanding and trying to get attention, to do the truth
quietly without display, to let the dishonesties in our lives fade away, to accept our
limitations, to cling to the gospel of grace, and to delight in your love. Amen.
—Brennan Manning

PRIORITY 11:

MAKE
YOUR BODY
A HOLY PLACE

MY
BODY
IS ABOUT HIM

EXPLORING

One thing is beyond dispute—our twenty-first-century Western culture is *body-obsessed*. Consider how many billions of dollars are spent annually by those who want . . .

- a *smaller* body (weight-loss plans, diet pills, low-fat or low carb foods)
- a *different* body (the mushrooming plastic surgery phenomenon)
- a more *toned* or *muscular* body (health clubs, home gyms, other exercise equipment, the proliferation of steroid use)
- *bodily pleasures* (gourmet foods to tantalize the taste buds, hot tubs and massages to soothe tired muscles, legal medications to numb pain, illegal drugs to bring pleasure, rampant sexual experimentation, and so forth)
- to gawk at *naked* bodies (the exploding pornography plague)
- to *decorate* their bodies (hair care, nail care, skin care, fashion, and make-up, tattooing, body piercing, and so forth).

What do you make of these trends? What does this obsession with our bodies say about us as a people?

_____

_____

_____

Do *you* work out? If so, what is your exercise regimen?

_____

_____

_____

When in your life were you in the best physical shape?

_____
_____
_____
_____
_____
_____
_____
_____

Do you "eat to live" or "live to eat"? What's the difference?

_____
_____
_____
_____
_____
_____
_____
_____
_____

How much value do you put on how your body looks?

_____
_____
_____
_____
_____
_____
_____
_____
_____

REFLECTING

In *It's Not About Me*, Max uses an analogy involving brazen house sitters. How do you think you would respond if such a person trashed your home? Or if while you were on vacation, a neighbor arbitrarily began renovating and redecorating to suit his or her tastes?

_____

_____

_____

Max speaks of the attitudes and practices of the first century Corinthian Christians:

"When it came to the body, they insisted, 'We can do anything we want to' (1 Corinthians 6:12 CEV). Their philosophy conveniently separated flesh from spirit. Have fun with the flesh. Honor God with the spirit. Wild Saturdays. Worshipful Sundays. You can have it all."

How prevalent is this mindset today among people in the church?

_____

_____

_____

The Bible tells us: "You are no longer your own. God paid a great price for you. So use your body to honor God" (1 Corinthians 6:19–20 CEV).

According to this passage, who holds the title deed to our lives? If we really believed this today, in what ways would we alter our activities?

_____

_____

_____

Max cites the command:

"Use your whole body as a tool to do what is right for the glory of God" (Romans 6:13 NLT).

What does it mean to use one's body as a tool for God? What are some specific ways a person can do this?

_____

_____

_____

Speaking to his followers, Jesus said:

> "And I will pray the Father, and He will give you another Helper, that He may abide with you forever" (John 14:16 NKJV, emphasis added).

In speaking of "another Helper," Jesus was referring to the Holy Spirit, who, beginning at Pentecost, would indwell all believers. That's what *abide* means: To indwell. To live in. To settle down and make oneself at home. In past generations people spoke of the house in which they resided as their "abode." It's the same root word. To *abide* in a place means to make that place your *abode*. In short, Jesus was saying, "In the person of the Holy Spirit. I'm going to make my home inside each and every person who believes in me." Amazing, eh? You and I are the dwelling place of Jesus. Our hearts are his home! Wow! It's enough to make you fall right out of your chair! No wonder Paul asked: "Don't you know that your body is the temple of the Holy Spirit, who lives in you?" (1 Corinthians 6:19 NLT).

Look at it this way—if you found out that an important dignitary was coming to stay at your home, what would you do to get ready?

_____

_____

_____

Why don't we work that hard to make ourselves—our lives, our hearts, our bodies—a fit home for Christ?

_____

_____

_____

That's enough to think about for now. Until next time, meditate on this transforming truth:

> "You are no longer your own. God paid a great price for you. So use your body to honor God" (1 Corinthians 6:19–20 CEV).

MAKING
YOUR BODY
A HOLY PLACE

REVIEWING

We've been thinking and discussing how Christians can (and should) use their bodies to bring honor to Jesus Christ. In the first part of Priority 11 we focused on the truth that we belong to God. He bought us; therefore he owns us.

Life is not about us—it's all about him. No wonder the Bible says, "Use your whole body as a tool to do what is right for the glory of God" (Romans 6:13 NLT).

To begin thinking practically about this issue, let's visit with John B. He's only 47 years old, but doctors recently told him that he has the body of someone 30 years *older*! Here's what this jovial man admitted:

Q: John, what is your precise medical condition?

A: Precise? Whew! (laughing) How much time do we have? Let's see (patting his enormous belly), I'm obviously overweight—too much good country cooking, I guess. And I've got high blood pressure. Oh, and I'm diabetic. Plus, I have emphysema—no doubt from smoking all those years.

Q: That's quite a list.

A: Yeah, and that's not everything either. I had some heart blockage last year. They had to do one of those "balloon" procedures, angioplasty, and that seemed to help.

Q: So you're on lots of medication?

A: (smiling) I take enough pills every day to gag a horse—about twenty-five every morning and another fifteen pills every night.

Q: You seem to take it all in stride and haven't lost your sense of humor.

A: Well, if you don't laugh, you'll cry—know what I mean? But seriously, I have regrets. Bottom line, I just haven't taken care of myself. And it's finally caught up with me. My wife has been on me for years. She says, "You take better care of that truck out there than you do your own self." And she's right. Isn't that crazy? I only put the best gas and oil in my truck, but up until a couple months ago, I'd put *anything and everything* in my body.

Now I've got grandkids and I can't even get out and play with them. Their memory of me will probably be of me sitting in this easy chair. I hate that. I also had to go inactive as a deacon at church. I just can't do all those projects anymore. Too strenuous. I hate that, too.

Q: So what's the prognosis?

A: No one knows for sure. I'm finally trying to eat right, eat healthy. Low-fat and all (winking and whispering), but sometimes I still cheat. I don't know—the Lord might keep my old heart ticking another fifty years or he might call me home next week. I guess that's true for all of us.

But if you're asking me for advice, I'd say think twice about how you treat your body. Because if you don't take care of it, it *will* wear out quicker, and you won't be able to serve the good Lord near as well. That's just the way life works.

Why do some folks take meticulous care of their vehicles or homes or gardens or pets, and give little or no thought to the careful maintenance of their bodies?

_____

_____

_____

On a scale of 1–10, with 1 = "Gone to the dogs" and 10 = "A finely tuned instrument," how well are you currently taking care of your body?

_____

_____

_____

What are a few things you could do to take better care of your body?

_____

_____

_____

EVALUATING

It's not good to let our bodies go, but what about the opposite extreme—what about fitness fanatics who spend countless hours each week engaging in physical exercise? What did Paul mean when he counseled: "Workouts in the gymnasium are useful, but a disciplined life in God is far more so, making you fit both today and forever" (1 Timothy 4:8 THE MESSAGE)?

_____

_____

_____

In his audio message, Max mentions 2 Timothy 2:20–21 (NLT):

> "In a wealthy home some utensils are made of gold and silver, and some are made of wood and clay. The expensive utensils are used for special occasions, and the cheap ones are for everyday use. If you keep yourself pure, you will be a utensil God can use for his purpose. Your life will be clean, and you will be ready for the Master to use you for every good work."

According to this passage, what kind of person does God use?

_____

_____

_____

Max quotes this verse:

> "Run away from sexual sin! No other sin so clearly affects the body as this one does. For sexual immorality is a sin against your own body" (1 Corinthians 6:18 NLT).

How is it that sexual sin affects the body more than other kinds of sin?

_____

_____

_____

What would you say to the common claim, "Sex is no big deal; it's just a physical act"?

_____

_____

_____

Is God anti-sex? How do you know? Why do you think God made sexual intimacy feel so amazing?

_____

_____

_____

While many have experienced the painful deceptions of inappropriate sex, Max reminds us of God's design for intimacy, "Sex according to God's plan nourishes the soul. Consider his plan. Two children of God make a covenant with each other. They disable the ejection seats. They burn the bridge back to Momma's house. They fall into each other's arms beneath the canopy of God's blessing, encircled by the tall fence of fidelity. Both know the other will be there in the morning. Both know the other will stay even as skin wrinkles and vigor fades."

> *"Your body, God's tool.*
> *Maintain it.*
> *Your body, God's temple.*
> *Respect it."*
>
> —Max Lucado

Paul writes, "Don't you know that your body is the temple of the Holy Spirit, who lives in you and was given to you by God? You do not belong to yourself, for God bought you with a high price. So you must honor God with your body" (1 Corinthians 6:19-20 NLT). When outsiders look at how you maintain your body and what you use it for, are they attracted to God or repelled?

_____

_____

_____

Contrast the behavior that might accompany the belief, "My body is mine, so I can do whatever I want with it," with the likely actions of the person who believes, "Since God owns my body, I will use it to honor him."

_____

_____

_____

CHANGING

What do you sense God is saying to you in this lesson about how to view your body?

_____

_____

_____

What steps can you take to use your body for God and his purposes?

_____

_____

_____

A *quote* for getting a right perspective on the physical and spiritual.

"Our Lord finds our desires not too strong, but too weak. We are half-hearted creatures, fooling about with drink and sex and ambition when infinite joy is offered us, like an ignorant child who wants to go on making mud pies in a slum because he cannot imagine what is meant by the offer of a holiday at the sea. We are far too easily pleased."
—C. S. Lewis

An *exercise* for realizing how much we are governed by bodily urges.

Unless you have medical issues that prevent you from doing so, try fasting* for 24 hours. Use the times you would normally eat to focus on God.

*Fasting, in the strict sense, means not eating food and drinking only water. Fasting can be dangerous for some people, so check with your doctor if you have questions.

As a spiritual discipline, fasting teaches much. It reveals how many of our thoughts and actions are centered around food and dictated by physical urges. It helps us come to grips with the almost extinct practice of self-denial (saying "no"). It forces us to cling to God and depend on him. And it causes us to be thankful for the food God does give. Remember Jesus' example: he believed so strongly in bringing our bodies under submission that he fasted for forty days before he began his earthly ministry. He consistently modeled self denial as the path to intimacy with God. As such, we're called to deny ourselves, take up our cross, and follow him.

Note: If you fast for twenty-four hours, you will *not* starve. Most likely you *will* experience sharp hunger pangs. Your stomach will growl fiercely. Your pampered body (which is accustomed to controlling your thoughts and actions and dictating your schedule) will rebel, demanding to be fed, now! If you drink a lot of water, you will feel less hungry, and you will flush out your system (a good thing!).

How do you feel about even the mere suggestion of fasting?

_____

_____

_____

If you attempt this exercise, use the space below to record your impressions.

_____

_____

_____

_____

_____

_____

_____

_____

_____

_____

A *prayer* for making your body a holy place.

Take my life and let it be
Consecrated, Lord, to Thee;
Take my hands and let them move
At the impulse of Thy love,
At the impulse of Thy love.

Take my feet and let them be
Swift and beautiful for Thee;
Take my voice and let me sing
Always, only, for my King,
Always, only, for my King.
—Francis R. Havergal

PRIORITY 12:

USE YOUR
SUFFERING
FOR GLORY

MY STRUGGLES
ARE ABOUT HIM

EXPLORING

We've all heard of the famous Murphy's Law—"Anything that can go wrong will go wrong." Did you know there are numerous elaborations of this general principle and related rules? For example:

- If anything simply cannot go wrong, it will anyway.
- If there is a possibility of several things going wrong, the one that will cause the most damage will be the one to go wrong.
- If you determine that there are four possible ways in which a procedure can go wrong, and you manage to circumvent these, then a fifth way, unprepared for, will promptly develop.
- If everything seems to be going well, you have obviously overlooked something.
- It is impossible to make anything foolproof because fools are so ingenious.
- Every solution breeds new problems.
- Nothing is as easy as it looks.
- Everything takes longer than you think.

And here are more "laws" about the way the world works:

- *Babcock's Law:* If it can be borrowed and it can be broken, you will borrow it and you will break it.
- *The Law of Copy Machines:* The legibility of a photocopy is inversely proportional to its importance.
- *The Law of Buttered Bread:* The chance of the bread falling with the buttered side down is directly proportional to the cost of the carpet.
- *The Law of the Workshop:* Any tool, when dropped, will roll into the least accessible corner of the workshop. Corollary: Any dropped tool will first always strike your toes.
- *Lynch's Law:* When the going gets tough, everybody leaves.
- *Young's Law:* All great discoveries are made by mistake. Corollary: The greater the funding, the longer it takes to make the mistake.

- *Wolf's Law of History Lessons:* Those who don't study the past will repeat its errors. Those who do study it will find other ways to err.
- *Parkin's Law of Irritation:* Anything that happens enough times to irritate you will happen at least once more.
- *Law of Human Nature:* Tell a man there are 300 billion stars in the universe, and he'll believe you. Tell him a bench has wet paint on it, and he'll have to touch it to be sure.
- *O'Toole's Commentary:* Murphy was an optimist.

What other Murphy-like laws and struggles have you discovered?

_____

_____

_____

_____

_____

_____

Why are some people laid back and able to flex and adapt (and perhaps even laugh) in the face of difficulties, while others just come unglued? Which kind of person are you?

_____

_____

_____

_____

_____

_____

Do you agree that life is filled with frustrations, and that nobody breezes through this world without problems and struggles? Why or why not?

_____

_____

_____

_____

_____

_____

REFLECTING

InMax notes that God allows or orchestrates certain trials in our lives in order that we might show-case his glory. What are your reactions to this notion?

_____

_____

_____

_____

Skeptics have argued that a loving and kind Creator *would* stop evil. However, their reasoning goes, since suffering and tragedies continue unabated in this often cruel world, either God isn't truly good, or—perhaps—he simply doesn't exist. Comment on this argument and logic. Do you agree or not?

_____

_____

_____

_____

Read the following Bible passage.

> "GOD is sheer mercy and grace;
> not easily angered, he's rich in love.
> He doesn't endlessly nag and scold,
> nor hold grudges forever.
> He doesn't treat us as our sins deserve,
> nor pay us back in full for our wrongs.
> As high as heaven is over the earth,
> so strong is his love to those who fear him."
> (Psalm 103:8–11 THE MESSAGE)

How does this contradict the notion that God is angry or vengeful, or anything less than good?

_____

_____

_____

_____

Another way some have tried to explain the fact of suffering is to portray God as not fully in control, and that at some level he is incapable of preventing all evil. How do you respond to this theory?

_____

_____

_____

_____

God is quoted in the psalms as saying, "Trust me in your times of trouble, and I will rescue you, and you will give me glory" (Psalm 50:15 NLT). This verse bluntly acknowledges the reality of trouble, but it also suggests the possibility of what?

_____

_____

_____

_____

Do you think your overall response during your last big "trial" glorified God? Why or why not?

_____

_____

_____

_____

How do you react when you observe someone exude genuine peace and joy in the midst of a world of trouble?

_____

_____

_____

_____

Someone has suggested that apart from faith, we will never be able to reconcile God's absolute goodness, perfect wisdom, and infinite power with the suffering we face. Do you agree? Why or why not?

_____

_____

_____

_____

John of the Cross was a sixteenth-century Spanish mystic, best known for his classic book The Dark Night of the Soul. *Spend a few minutes pondering some of his thoughts:*

"See that you are not suddenly saddened by the adversities of this world, for you do not know the good they bring, being ordained in the judgments of God for the everlasting joy of the elect."

"He who seeks not the cross of Christ seeks not the glory of Christ."

"Never give up in prayer; and should you find dryness and difficulty, persevere in it for this very reason. God often desires to see what love your soul has, and love is not tried by ease and satisfaction."

"Well and good if all things change, Lord God, provided we are rooted in You."

As we come to the end of the first part of this study, spend some time wrestling with this question: What's more common in your life—pursuing relief from life's problems or pursuing God in the midst of problems and promoting his righteous reputation, no matter what?

_____

_____

_____

_____

_____

USING YOUR
SUFFERING
FOR GLORY

REVIEWING

This is the second half of an important discussion of Priority 12 on *difficulty and suffering*. Why does God allow us to experience pain and hardship? How should we handle those problems? What do those hardships have to do with God? Most importantly, can we really use our trials and afflictions to bring God glory?

Here are some important points to note:

- Follow our troubles to their headwaters, and you won't find an angry or befuddled God. But you will find a sovereign God.
- Your pain has a purpose. Your problems, struggles, heartaches, and hassles cooperate toward one end—the glory of God"
- Your faith in the face of suffering cranks up the volume of God's song.
- Is there any chance . . . that you have been selected to struggle for God's glory?
- A season of suffering is a small assignment when compared to the reward.
- Rather than begrudge your problem, explore it. Ponder it.
- And most of all, use it. Use it to the glory of God.

That's a lot to process. Maybe a real-life story can help bring these truths into focus:

"*Merry* Christmas" and a "*Happy* New Year"?

Maybe it would be best *not* to express such sentiments to Kathi this coming yuletide season. You see, it was last December 23—at the height of the holidays—that Kathi learned her husband, Bill, was having an affair with a gorgeous grad student at the local university.

She was understandably hurt, sad, and angry. A million thoughts ran through her head—divorce, suicide, even homicide! But after a week away at her parents' beach house, she stunned a lot of people by announcing she was going to do whatever it took to save her marriage.

Over the next few months, a number of things changed for the better. Kathi quit her stressful job. Bill made the effort to be at home more. The couple began attending church together and seeing a marriage counselor weekly. Kathi even lost thirty pounds and began attending a ladies' prayer group in the neighborhood.

But then, everything unraveled again. Doing some laundry, Kathi found a university parking ticket in Bill's jeans. When she quizzed him, he said he had been on campus to see a baseball game. But when Kathi checked around, his alibi didn't add up. Several hours later, a "cornered" Bill tearfully admitted that he had fallen off the fidelity wagon again. He begged forgiveness and pleaded for another chance. But Kathi literally kicked him out the house, hurling his belongings onto the front driveway.

Today Kathi is still fuming:

"Of course I'm angry! And depressed and scared and wounded. But mostly mad. I'm so angry at Bill, I can't see straight! I'm ticked at myself for being so naïve and stupid! And you know what else? I realize I'm mad at God. Frankly, I feel betrayed. I've been trying my dead-level best to do everything right—the diet, church, counseling. I haven't missed a single day reading the Bible and praying. Not one! And for what? What good did all that do? Here we are right back where we were in January. Nothing has changed. In fact, if anything, the situation is worse now. So don't tell me that God blesses those who live right. It's just not true. I kept my end of the bargain. God is the one who didn't keep his word! I feel abandoned. Tricked. Stupid."

When have you felt the way Kathi does? How did you handle it?

_____

_____

_____

Read between the lines. What were Kathi's unspoken thoughts and assumptions these last few months? What were her expectations? Are these legitimate?

_____

_____

_____

What is the difference between consciously *hoping* that God will do something to change our suffering, and subconsciously *demanding* that he do something?

_____

_____

_____

Given where Kathi and Bill are right now, how can God receive glory in their lives and marriage?

_____

_____

_____

EVALUATING

Max notes two stories in the Bible that illustrate suffering fro God's glory. The first involves a man chosen by God for blindness:

> "As [Jesus] passed by, He saw a man who was blind from birth. And His disciples asked Him, 'Rabbi, who sinned, this man or his parents, that he was born blind?' Jesus answered, 'Neither this man nor his parents sinned, but that the works of God should be revealed in him' " (John 9:1–3 NKJV).

The second involves a seriously ill man, allowed by Jesus to die:

> "But when Jesus heard [about illness of Lazarus], He said, 'This sickness is not unto death, but for the glory of God, so that the Son of God may be glorified through it.'
>
> Now Jesus loved Martha and her sister and Lazarus. So, when He heard that he was sick, He stayed two more days in the place where He was" (John 11:4–6 NKJV).

What's your gut reaction to these accounts?

_____

_____

_____

How would you like to trade places with the blind man? How would you like to be Mary or Martha, knowing that Jesus deliberately allowed your brother to die? Explain your response.

_____

_____

_____

Philippians 1:29 (NIV) tells us, "For it has been granted to you on behalf of Christ not only to believe on him, but also to suffer for him." Why should those who follow Christ not be surprised to encounter difficulties and tough times?

_____

_____

_____

What is the biggest ordeal you've ever faced? The greatest tragedy?

_____

_____

_____

Which of the following best describes your usual response to life's difficulties (check all that apply):

_____ I live in denial.
_____ I look for some kind of escape, diversion, amusement, or way to "medicate" my discomfort.
_____ I whine a lot.
_____ I grit my teeth and try to gut it out.
_____ I blame God.
_____ I blame others.
_____ I blame myself.
_____ I blame the devil.
_____ I thank God.
_____ Other: specify_____

In what tough situation are you currently finding it difficult to live for God's glory?

_____

_____

_____

How would you respond if an irreligious friend were to ask you, "Why does God allow his people to experience such hardship and suffering?"

_____

_____

_____

CHANGING

Okay, God can get glory through our suffering. Not a fun thought. But what about us? What possible benefits can come to us from hardship? (Hint: See Romans 5:1–5 and 8:28–29.)

_____

_____

_____

Corrie ten Boom once said: "When the train goes through a tunnel and the world gets dark, do you jump out? Of course not. You sit still and trust the engineer to get you through." Why is it so difficult to sit still and wait on God in tough times? In what scary or tough situations do you need to "trust the engineer" today?

_____

_____

_____

What's the single most significant lesson or truth you've learned so far in this study, and why?

_____

_____

_____

From now until the next lesson, consider:

A *story* about using your suffering for God's glory.

In his book *Disappointment with God*, Philip Yancey tells about a teenager named Peggie. She was afflicted with cystic fibrosis and was dying a slow, agonizing death. But then she heard her minister say, "Endurance is more than just the ability to bear a hard thing; it's also the resolve to turn that suffering into glory."

A short time later, Yancey says, when her condition worsened, Peggie looked about her hospital room "at all the paraphernalia of death to which she was attached." Then she reminded her mom of the preacher's words about enduring and turning suffering to glory. She "stuck the tip of her tongue out of the corner of her mouth, nodded her head, and raised her eyes in excitement at the experiment to which she was committing herself."

She was deciding to glorify God no matter what. And those who knew her say she never wavered and she never complained, not a single time, even during her final horrible days.

A *quote* about the purpose of suffering.

> **"We must offer ourselves to God like . . . a piece of stone. Each blow from the sculptor's chisel makes it feel—if it could—as if it were being destroyed. As blow upon blow descends, the stone knows nothing of how the sculptor is shaping it. All it feels is a chisel chopping away at it, cutting it, and mutilating it. . . . [I]t might [say]: 'I have no idea what he is doing, nor do I know what he will make of me. But I know his work is the best possible. It is perfect, and so I welcome each blow of his chisel as the best thing that could happen to me, although, if I'm to be truthful, I feel that every one of these blows is ruining me, destroying me, and disfiguring me.'"**
> —Jean Pierre de Caussade

An *exercise* for putting suffering in perspective.

Take some time to meditate on the apostle Paul's experience as recorded in 2 Corinthians 4:8–18 (NLT).

> *"We are pressed on every side by troubles, but we are not crushed and broken. We are perplexed, but we don't give up and quit. We are hunted down, but God never abandons us. We get knocked down, but we get up again and keep going. Through suffering, these bodies of ours constantly share in the death of Jesus so that the life of Jesus may also be seen in our bodies.*
>
> *Yes, we live under constant danger of death because we serve Jesus, so that the life of Jesus will be obvious in our dying bodies. So we live in the face of death, but it has resulted in eternal life for you.*
>
> *But we continue to preach because we have the same kind of faith the psalmist had when he said, 'I believed in God, and so I speak.' We know that the same God who raised our Lord Jesus will also raise us with Jesus and present us to himself along with you. All of these things are for your benefit. And as God's grace brings more and more people to Christ, there will be great thanksgiving, and God will receive more and more glory.*
>
> *That is why we never give up. Though our bodies are dying, our spirits are being renewed every day. For our present troubles are quite small and won't last very long. Yet they produce for us an immeasurably*

great glory that will last forever! So we don't look at the troubles we can see right now; rather, we look forward to what we have not yet seen. For the troubles we see will soon be over, but the joys to come will last forever."

Summarize how Paul viewed his struggles and hardships. What were the results?

_____

_____

_____

How can you walk through your immediate hardships in a way that glorifies God?

_____

_____

_____

How can you be an instrument of compassion and encouragement in the lives of loved ones to help them glorify God in their hardships?

_____

_____

_____

A *reminder* to keep praying in hard times.

"The one thing you can be sure of is that . . . the God you call upon will finally come, and even if he does not bring you the answer you want, he will bring you himself. And maybe at the secret heart of all our prayers that is what we are really praying for."
—Frederick Buechner

PRIORITY 13:

REDEFINE
YOUR IDEA
OF SUCCESS

MY
SUCCESS
IS ABOUT HIM

EXPLORING

How do you define *success*? Does it mean having a lot of money? Being a prominent person in your field? Accomplishing great feats and receiving acclaim for your exploits?

Does success mean having great influence? Or achieving certain personal goals? How about enjoying a big circle of family and friends?

Take a few minutes now to ponder your own attitudes and values when it comes to this topic of success by doing the following "Success Shopping Spree."

SUCCESS SHOPPING SPREE

Instructions: You may spend up to $100 (but not a penny more). Check the items you think would give you the greatest sense of attainment and triumph in life. Note: Shop wisely!

Items costing $25:

_____ an intimate and fulfilling relationship with Jesus Christ, marked by otherworldly peace and joy

_____ a close-knit family that genuinely loves to be together and enjoys rich, fun times of building memories

_____ an immensely satisfying career that fits with my deepest passions and utilizes to the full all my gifts and abilities

_____ a rare, highly-valued ability; the chance to be among the world's best in a certain skill or activity (like Tiger Woods in golf or Meryl Streep in acting)

_____ a rich and wonderful marriage where we become true soulmates

Items costing $20:

_____ a circle of lifelong, true friends, and close relationships marked by love and acceptance, encouragement and laughter

_____ membership in an amazing, dynamic, influential church—a bona fide "spiritual family"

_____ excellent health and a long, energetic, productive life

_____ financial prosperity—the monetary resources to do things most people only dream of

_____ fame (being a household name—having celebrity status)

Items costing $15:

_____ opportunities to introduce many people to Christ and help them grow in their faith

_____ a world-class education from a prestigious "Top Five" university

_____ ownership of my own business and seeing it grow, prosper, and win accolades

_____ children who grow up to find their niche in life and who establish godly, happy marriages and homes

Items costing $10:

_____ being able to build and furnish my dream home in my preferred location

_____ being able to get and keep the body I've always dreamed of

_____ being able to send my children to the best schools and see them enter highly respected fields

_____ being able to retire early

Items costing $5:

_____ a passel of grandchildren

_____ ample time to pursue my hobbies and avocations (and do them well!)

_____ the opportunity to travel first-class wherever and whenever I wish

_____ membership in certain clubs and organizations

What did you like about this exercise?

_____

_____

_____

What did you dislike about this exercise?

_____

_____

_____

How can an exercise like this be enlightening or helpful?

_____

_____

_____

_____

REFLECTING

In _It's Not About Me_, Max talked about advertising agencies and some of their most effective campaigns. Were you familiar with the names of those ad agencies? What was Max's point?

_____

_____

_____

_____

Just for fun (and before we move on), what TV commercial(s) would you deem as the best, most creative, most memorable, and most effective? Why?

_____

_____

_____

_____

Okay, this is no time for false modesty—what are _your_ talents? What awards have you received? What blessings (relational, occupational, financial, physical) do you enjoy?

_____

_____

_____

_____

What have been your greatest successes in life? Why?

_____

_____

_____

Max quotes these Bible passages:

"Always remember that it is the LORD your God who gives you power to become rich, and he does it to fulfill the covenant he made with your ancestors" (Deuteronomy 8:18 NLT).

"Riches and honor come from you alone, for you rule over everything. Power and might are in your hand, and it is at your discretion that people are made great and given strength" (1 Chronicles 29:12 NLT).

"They did not conquer the land with their swords; it was not their own strength that gave them victory. It was by your mighty power that they succeeded; it was because you favored them and smiled on them" (Psalm 44:3 NLT).

According to these passages, who or what is the source of all human success?

_____

_____

_____

In Hosea 13:4–6 (NLT), God chastises his people for letting the blessings he provided go to their heads:

"I am the LORD your God, who rescued you from your slavery in Egypt. You have no God but me, for there is no other savior. I took care of you in the wilderness, in that dry and thirsty land. But when you had eaten and were satisfied, then you became proud and forgot me."

What is *pride*? How would you define it to a child?

_____

_____

_____

PONDERING THE PERIL OF PRIDE

"Pride goes before destruction, and haughtiness before a fall" (Proverbs 16:18 NLT).

"The essential vice, the utmost evil, is Pride. . . . It was through Pride that the devil became the devil. Pride leads to every other vice; it is the complete anti-God state of mind. . . . In God you come up against something which is in every respect immeasurably superior to yourself. Unless you know God as that—and, therefore, know yourself as nothing in comparison—you do not know God at all. As long as you are proud you cannot know God. A proud man is always looking down on things and people; and, of course, as long as you are looking down, you cannot see something that is above you."

—C. S. Lewis

Max tells this story:

"A frog's home pond was drying up. If he didn't find water soon, he would do the same. Word reached him of a vibrant stream over the adjacent hill. If only he could live there. But how could he? The short legs of a frog were not made for long journeys.

"But then he had an idea. Convincing two birds to carry either end of a stick, he bit the center and held on as they flew. As they winged toward the new water, his jaws clamped tightly. It was quite a sight! Two birds, one stick, and a frog in the middle. Down below, a cow in a pasture saw them passing over head. Impressed, he wondered aloud. 'Now who came up with that idea?'

"The frog overheard his question and couldn't resist a reply. 'I diiiiii . . .'"

What's the moral of the story?

_____

_____

_____

_____

How are you redefining your idea of what true success is?

_____

_____

_____

_____

REDEFINING
YOUR IDEA
OF SUCCESS

REVIEWING

Welcome to the conclusion of our study of success and Priority 13. Why does God allow us to prosper? And why do some people seem to enjoy so much more success than others? Why are we given certain talents and abilities? Is it to bask in the affirmation and applause of others? Is it to enable us to poke out our chests and parade about, to the envy of others?

Here are some important points to remember:

- God lets you excel so you can make him known.
- Why did God help you succeed? So you can make him known.
- Success sabotages the memories of the successful. Kings of the mountain forget who carried them up the trail.
- Why are you good at what you do? For God's sake. Your success is not about what you do. It's all about him—his present and future glory.

Perhaps these first person accounts will help us personalize these truths:

Dr. Ellen M. (a heart surgeon):

"I don't remember the exact sequence of events. Things were very busy and very good. I had good people working for me—a competent office staff, a good O.R. team. We were doing lots of procedures. The stock market was roaring and all my investments were paying off. It was a good time financially. The kids were doing well academically in a really good private school. Then we built this beautiful house. I mean, you want to talk about everything coming together? It was unbelievable.

"I guess it was sometime during the move that I came across the box filled with my old journals from med school. I started reading back over what I had written, and it was quite humbling. That had been such a tough time of my life, yet my relationship with God was vibrant. I mean, I was hanging on to God and pleading for help and praying all the time that he would just me get through. Prayers such as: 'O God, I really want to serve you through medicine. I want to help people. I want my career to be a ministry.' And I *really* meant every word.

"It seemed that that was some kind of wake-up call. Maybe God reminding me, 'Don't forget me. Don't forget that *I'm* the One who got you to this place. What about your promise to use your skills and your resources for me?'

"Why are we like that? Why do we forget so quickly?"

*　*　*　*　*

Bill D. (a deacon in his church):

"Our church was going through a really tough time; in fact, it wasn't certain that we would survive. Our pastor had admitted to being in an immoral relationship. He left, and a bunch of folks left in support of him. We had just completed an expensive building program. We were left with this huge note, and didn't know how we were going to pay it.

"Well, what else could we do? We prayed like we never had prayed before. Daily. Every morning a group of men would gather up at the church. Some of the women started an around-the-clock prayer chain.

"I'm telling you, it was something. Out of all that mess, God brought blessing and healing like never before—new folks joining the church and people giving. We weathered the storm and found a new pastor everyone really likes. Our church is blowing and going.

"But here's the truth plain and simple—we don't pray much any more. That sense of desperation is gone. God got us through the rough times, and now we act like we can handle things just fine all by ourselves. Sort of like what happened in the country after 9-11."

Compare these two stories. What's the common thread in both? What's different?

_____

_____

_____

When have you had a similar experience of vacillating trust and dependence?

_____

_____

_____

EVALUATING

In *It's Not About Me*, Max relates the fable of an elephant lumbering across a wooden bridge suspended over a ravine. As the big animal crossed over, the worn-out structure creaked and groaned under the elephant's weight. When he reached the other side, a flea that had nestled itself in the elephant's ear proclaimed, "Boy, did we shake that bridge!"

What's wrong with the flea's perspective? How is this an apt illustration of the way we often think and act?

_____

_____

_____

The Old Testament book of Proverbs is loaded with principles for living and wise sayings about the way the world typically works. Proverbs 22:4 says: "True humility and fear of the LORD lead to riches, honor, and long life" (NLT).

What does "true humility and fear of the Lord" look like in a person's everyday life?

_____

_____

_____

Someone has said, "Humility is not looking at yourself badly, it is not looking at yourself *at all*." Do you agree with this description? Why or why not?

_____

_____

_____

Okay, true confessions time. When you succeed at something (whatever "success" happens to look like in your life), are you quick to lift your eyes heavenward and acknowledge your blessing as coming from God? Do you thank him? Or do you gloat and strut about, forgetting him?

_____

_____

_____

Do you tend to see your achievements as the work of your hands? As your own doing? The result of your own intelligence and hard work? Why or why not?

_____

_____

_____

Through the prophet Zechariah, God reminded Zerubbabel, the leader of the Jews returning to the promised land from Babylonian captivity, how and why they were guaranteed to prosper:

> "So he said to me, 'This is the word of the LORD to Zerubbabel: 'Not by might nor by power, but by my Spirit,' says the LORD Almighty" (Zechariah 4:6 NIV).

How is this verse a good reminder for us today?

_____

_____

_____

Remember Max's words:

"Why are you good at what you do? For your comfort? For your retirement? For your self-esteem? No. Deem these as bonuses, not as the reason. Why are you good at what you do? For God's sake. Your success is not about what you do. It's all about him—his present and future glory."

CHANGING

Success is a relative term. You may not have as much power, wealth, or intelligence as some people, but you do have more than other people. At issue isn't the nature of our success or how much we perceive that we have or don't have. No, the real issue is what will we do with the good things God has done in us and for us.

What specific changes do you sense you need to make in your life as a result of this study . . .

In how you _think_ about success?

_____

_____

_____

In how you *speak* about success?

_____

_____

_____

In how you *act* over success?

_____

_____

_____

In how you *pray* about success?

_____

_____

_____

Author and pastor M. Craig Barnes observed: "You can either try to achieve a life or you can receive a life. One makes you upset that it's not good enough, and the other makes you grateful for what you've been given." Do you think he's right? What's the difference between achieving and receiving?

_____

_____

_____

How can you use your God-ordained achievements to showcase God?

_____

_____

_____

How can you use your accomplishments to talk about God in a way that doesn't sound fake or pious?

_____

_____

_____

A *quote* for redefining your idea of success.

> "Remember always that everything that happens to you, whether prosperous
> or adverse, comes from God, so that you neither become puffed up
> in prosperity nor discouraged in adversity."
> —John of the Cross

An *exercise* for developing a more thankful and less prideful heart.

In the space below, make a list of all the good gifts God has dropped into your life—all the blessings, all the ways he has shown you favor. Then go through your list carefully, item by item, thanking God for each entry, and asking him to help you use that experience or expertise or possession or relationship for his glory.

_____

_____

_____

A *prayer* for remembering to glorify God in all our blessings and in each success.

> "Not to us, O LORD, not to us but to your name be the glory,
> because of your love and faithfulness.
>
> Why do the nations say, 'Where is their God?' Our God is in heaven; he does whatever pleases him. But their idols are silver and gold, made by the hands of men. They have mouths, but cannot speak, eyes, but they cannot see; they have ears, but cannot hear, noses, but they cannot smell; they have hands, but cannot feel, feet, but they cannot walk; nor can they utter a sound with their throats. Those who make them will be like them, and so will all who trust in them.
>
> O house of Israel, trust in the LORD—he is their help and shield. O house of Aaron, trust in the LORD—he is their help and shield. You who fear him, trust in the LORD—he is their help and shield. The LORD remembers us and will bless us: He will bless the house of Israel, he will bless the house of Aaron, he will bless those who fear the LORD—small and great alike.
>
> May the LORD make you increase, both you and your children. May you be blessed by the LORD, the Maker of heaven and earth.

The highest heavens belong to the Lord, but the earth he has given to man.
It is not the dead who praise the LORD, those who go down to silence;
it is we who extol the LORD, both now and forevermore.
Praise the LORD."
—Psalm 115 (NIV)

PRIORITY 14:

RETHINK
YOUR WAY
TO HAPPINESS

UPWARD
THINKING

EXPLORING

Surprise! In this final study, you get to host your very own awards show. Forget the Oscars, Tonys, Grammys, and Emmys—these are the *Best-ys*!

Your assignment is simple. Take five minutes to list some of the best people and things in your life. (If you are doing this study with a group, be prepared to share three Best-ys you awarded and why.)

- My best *friend* as a kid (ages 5–12):

- The best *job* I ever had:

- The best *pet* I ever had:

- The best *book* I ever read:

- The best *movie* I ever saw:

- The best *car* I ever drove:

- The best *vacation* I ever took:

- The best *class* I ever took in school:

- The best *boss* I ever had:

- The best *teacher* I ever had:

- The best *birthday* I ever remember:

- The best *place* I ever lived:

What are the five *best* adjectives (for example: kind, honest, and so forth) you *wish* people would use to describe your life?

_____

_____

_____

To date, what has been the best *moment* in your relationship with God? Why?

_____

_____

_____

REFLECTING

In *It's Not About Me*, Max tells of meeting a rabbi on a plane and getting a surprising lesson in what it means to "not take the Lord's name in vain." According to the rabbi, this command encompasses more than just what's on our *lips*; rather, it's all about the way we live our whole *lives*.

How have you usually interpreted and applied the command found in Exodus 20:7 to your life?

_____

_____

_____

Explain how gossiping or fudging on one's income taxes or being rude to a waitress are actually ways we "take the Lord's name in vain."

_____

_____

_____

What's the most challenging part of being a representative of God?

_____

_____

_____

Writing to some Christians in ancient Corinth, the apostle Paul said:

> *"We are therefore Christ's ambassadors, as though God were making his appeal through us"* (2 Corinthians 5:20 NIV).

What exactly do ambassadors do? Why are they important? How can a bad ambassador really make a mess of things?

_____

_____

_____

What's the job description for an "ambassador for Christ"?

_____

_____

_____

We've looked at this verse in a previous lesson, but it's worth examining again. 1 Corinthians 10:31 says: "Whatever you eat or drink or whatever you do, you must do all for the glory of God" (NLT). Consider your scheduled activities for the next couple of days. Thinking specifically, how does a person:

- *Sleep* for the glory of God?
- *Eat* for the glory of God?
- *Work* for the glory of God?
- *Exercise* for the glory of God?
- *Drive* for the glory of God?
- *Shop* for the glory of God?
- *Watch TV* for the glory of God?
- *Clean house* for the glory of God?

Which of these activities (or another one not listed) presents the biggest challenge to you, and why?

_____

_____

_____

How does living for God's glory help you rethink what it means to be happy and fulfilled?

_____

_____

_____

Before you come to the final session, spend a few minutes skimming back through this guidebook. Note your responses to various questions. What big themes jump out at you? What ideas keep grabbing your attention? What trends of needed growth in your life do you see?

_____

_____

_____

REFLECTING ON OUR REASON FOR BEING

"If any of us could be transported to heaven for even a five-minute visit, we would never be the same after our return to earth. For the first time, we would have a true perspective on the frailty and brevity of life on earth and the absurdity of giving our hearts to things that will not last."

—Ken Boa

"Worship is the submission of all our nature to God. It is the quickening of conscience by his holiness; the nourishment of mind with his truth; the purifying of imagination by his beauty; the opening of the heart to his love; the surrender of will to his purpose—and all of this gathered up in adoration, the most self-less emotion of which our nature is capable and therefore the chief remedy for that self-centeredness which is our original sin and the source of all actual sin."

—William Temple

"In all things, both high and low, let God be your goal."

—John of the Cross

RETHINKING
YOUR WAY
TO HAPPINESS

REVIEWING

Now we come to our final session, the last half of Priority 14. By now, the big idea of this study should be crystal clear. We exist to give honor to God's name. May we have no higher goal than to see someone think more highly of our Father, our king.

One last real-life situation can help us tie some of these final thoughts together:

Callie and her father are watching TV together—a special program about the lengths to which paparazzi will go in order to get snapshots of Hollywood's biggest stars.

"Can you imagine living like that, Dad? Every time you go out the door, somebody's hiding in the bushes to take your picture? You just want to run up to the convenience store and get a drink, but suddenly you have six people with cameras and microphones following you. There are weirdoes combing through your trash and writing stories in the tabloids about your likes and dislikes. Wow. I used to think I wanted to be famous—not anymore!"

Callie's father nods and smiles. "Fame is *not* all it's cracked up to be. But you know, even though we don't have photographers stalking us, we *do* have people watching us like hawks."

"What do you mean?"

"Well, think about it. You're active in the youth group. You go on a mission trip every summer. I lead a Bible study before work every Thursday morning. People watch us drive off to church every Sunday. In other words, it's no secret that we claim to be Christians. So, I guarantee you, people *are* watching us every day, to see if we really practice what we preach, to see if our faith is real."

"You think that's really true?"

"Oh, it *is* true, believe me. The things we say, the way we react to situations—good and bad—the way we treat people. Every day our neighbors and friends, your fellow students, my coworkers—they're all taking mental pictures and making mental notes. And either we are a good advertisement for the claims of Christ, or not. You know, there's one guy at work who preaches at everybody. He's always quoting the Bible and singing Christian songs. But you know what? He's actually kind of annoying. Loud. Abrasive. And lots of times he's just plain rude and insensitive to others."

"Really?!"

"Really. The bottom line is people don't like him, Callie. They talk about him behind his back. About what a hypocrite he is."

After a long silence, Callie says, "I guess the goal then is to live in such a way that when people do watch you and talk about you, they end up saying good stuff."

"Exactly. And not just good stuff about you. But good stuff about God."

Consider the statements of Callie's father. Do you agree or disagree that people watch what Christians do and say?

_____

_____

_____

Think of the Christians you know at work, school, or church. Whose life makes God look good? Why?

_____

_____

_____

EVALUATING

The Bible asserts that when a person believes in Christ, he or she becomes a new creature (2 Corinthians 5:17) and a true "child of God" (John 1:12). In other words, in a spiritual but very real sense, the person becomes a member of the ultimate "royal family."

So here's the question: How much of your heavenly Father's character does the world see in you? Are you helping or hindering God's reputation? How do you know?

_____

_____

_____

Let's get even more specific. Using the "fruit of the Spirit" (Galatians 5:22–23) as a kind of measuring stick, rate yourself on how well you are reflecting God's glorious nature to a watching world? Poorly, about average, or excellently? Circle the one that best fits.

	Poor				*Average*				*Excellent*	
Love	1	2	3	4	5	6	7	8	9	10
Joy	1	2	3	4	5	6	7	8	9	10
Peace	1	2	3	4	5	6	7	8	9	10
Patience	1	2	3	4	5	6	7	8	9	10
Kindness	1	2	3	4	5	6	7	8	9	10
Goodness	1	2	3	4	5	6	7	8	9	10
Faithfulness	1	2	3	4	5	6	7	8	9	10
Gentleness	1	2	3	4	5	6	7	8	9	10
Self-control	1	2	3	4	5	6	7	8	9	10

What can you do to bring up your scores in these areas?

_____

_____

_____

George Mueller, the nineteenth-century Christian noted for his ministry to orphans and his extraordinary faith once said: "I saw . . . that the first great and primary business to which I ought to attend every day was to have my soul happy in the Lord."

His point? True happiness is found only in surrendering ourselves completely to God's purposes, realizing that we have been created by him and for him and then living accordingly.

Would you say, at this moment in your life, your soul *is* happy in the Lord? Why or why not?

_____

_____

_____

Max says:

"The ambassador has a singular aim—to represent his king. He promotes the king's agenda, protects the king's reputation, and presents the king's will. The ambassador elevates the name of the king.

"Can I close . . . with a prayer that we do the same? May God rescue us from self-centered thinking. May we have no higher goal than to see someone think more highly of our Father, our king. After all, it's not about . . . well, you can finish the sentence."

CHANGING

A. W. Tozer once wrote: "[God] is by his nature continuously articulate. He fills the world with his speaking voice." How has he spoken to you during this study, as you've reflected on his Word and on your own life?

_____

_____

_____

One last time: Life is *not* about us. It's all about God. Our days are not about our comfort or desires, they are about God's glory. It's one thing to talk or study about such a way of life; living in this manner is a whole different issue.

What specific change do you need to make in your life today? How is the Lord prompting you? Think in terms of attitudes and actions that you need to either renounce or embrace.

_____

_____

_____

A *story* for remembering it's not about us; rather, it is about loving and serving him.

An elderly woman was ushered into President Abraham Lincoln's office. "What can I do for you?" he asked.

Placing a covered basket on his desk she replied softly, "Mr. President, I have come not to ask a favor for myself or anyone else. I heard you were very fond of cookies, so I came here simply to bring you this basket of cookies."

Tears trickled down the gaunt face of the President. "My dear woman, your thoughtful and unselfish deed has greatly moved me. Thousands have come into this office since I became President but you are the first one to come asking no favor for yourself."

How do you approach *God*—to get from him or to give to him? To ask for his blessing or to seek to bless him? He knows your needs before you even ask, but he delights in your appetite for his acclaim.

An *exercise* for rethinking your way to happiness.

In the space below, write a letter to God. Pour out your heart. Confess your failures, and embrace his forgiveness. Admit your deepest spiritual longings, and call upon his infinite power. Describe the kind of God-centered life you'd like to have, and claim the certain promises of Christ.

_____

_____

_____

A *prayer* for hearing God so that we might be doers of his Word and live wholly for him.

You speak, Lord, to all men in general through general events. Revolutions
are simply the tides of your Providence, which stir up storms and tempests in
people's minds. You speak to men in particular through particular events,
as they occur moment by moment.

But instead of hearing your voice, instead of respecting events as signals of your
loving guidance, people see nothing else but blind chance and human decision.
They find objections to everything you say. They wish to add or subtract
from your Word. They wish to change or reform it.

Teach me, dear Lord, to read clearly this book of life. I wish to be like a simple
child, accepting your word regardless of whether I understand
your purposes. It is enough for me that you speak.
—Jean-Pierre De Caussade

A final word from Max:

In our lives there are defining moments where we choose, as an act of the will,
to submit ourselves to God's scrutiny so that we can feel the warmth of his pleasure. You have
discarded pride for progress as you've worked through these priorities. Never forget, life is a
brief pause on this earth. And our greatest motivation must be the glory of our Lord. For in one
shining moment, all the trials and disappointments of this life will fade in the astounding words
of our Savior, "Well done, good and faithful servant." See you there.

APPENDIX

Using the *It's Not About Me Personal Guidebook* in a Group Setting

The *It's Not About Me Personal Guidebook* can be adapted for use in a group setting. The Introduction to this Guidebook will help you prepare by giving you an overview of the design of the course and the way the various components are used during each session. You will also rely on the Guidebook during each session.

For each session, the participants will need:

- Personal Guidebook
- Pen or pencil

You should also encourage your participants to purchase a copy (or have copies available for them to purchase) of the book *It's Not About Me* by Max Lucado.

The Design of the Program

Notice in the introduction to this Guidebook, under the section "How to Use This Program," that the program is divided into 14 sections called "Priorities." Each "Priority" is divided into two sessions (A and B) for a total of 28 individual sessions. Ideally we recommend that your group cover the material in 28 separate sessions. However, if you prefer, consider covering each "Priority" in one session, for a total of 14 sessions. In either case, it is highly recommended that you as the leader complete the 28 sessions on an individual basis prior to leading your group through the experience.

Leading Your Group

At their best, small group studies can foster learning, transparency, community, and even life change. Of course, not every session will achieve this pinnacle. That's OK. As a small group leader, you simply want to provide opportunities for people to engage in meaningful fellowship and discussion each week. Think of yourself as a facilitator—a conduit for the work God wants to do in your group; he is responsible for the end result. Expect to be surprised by the way he uses you.

As you prepare to lead a group through the *It's Not About Me Personal Guidebook*, here are a few suggestions to help you get started:

Pray often. Prayer will encourage you to rely on God and will sensitize you to the leading of his Spirit. So surround your efforts with prayer. Pray before, during, and after each session. Pray during the week for every person in your small group. If possible, devote time during the session for group members to pray for one another as well. You will find that prayer is the foundation on which God does his best work.

As you seek to pray regularly for yourself and for the members of your group, ask God to:

- Guide you in your preparation
- Guard the times set aside for each session, enabling group members to attend faithfully
- Penetrate the heart of every participant with specific truths they need to learn and apply
- Create an atmosphere of acceptance in the group, with opportunities to listen to and encourage one another
- Nurture group members in their private times with God throughout each week, using the studies to promote lasting spiritual growth in their lives

Take time to prepare. It is recommended that you complete the entire program on your own prior to leading your group through the course. If that is not possible, at the very least, spend a couple hours before every meeting going through the lesson on your own. Listen to the presentation by Max; read every section; answer every question; and enjoy the closing worship song. Pay close attention to those points in the session that catch your interest, challenge your presuppositions, and seem especially relevant to your group. Allow God to direct your mind during these times. After all, you've prayed and asked for his guidance!

Now go back through the lesson and choose the questions you want to be sure to go over as a group. (You may anticipate not being able to cover every question, so instead, focus on the ones that will best stimulate discussion and highlight the main points of each session. This will be especially important if you are covering the material in 14 sessions rather than 28.) It may be helpful to estimate how much time you would like to allot to each question or activity. Group members will appreciate studies that end on time and don't leave large sections of the lesson uncovered.

Lead with enthusiasm and sensitivity. The first session will lay the groundwork for what is to come, especially if your group has never met together before. So take some time to allow people to get to know one another. Seek to create a comfortable environment, setting the tone early for your future discussions. Encourage every person to give input, without neglecting those who are quieter or allowing those who are more outgoing to dominate.

As you settle into leading each week, keep these tips in mind:

Silence is okay. Instead of rushing to fill every quiet space with an answer or thought, allow people time to consider their responses. Sometimes the best discussions begin after a brief period of reflection. If the silence continues after you've allowed ample time for consideration, simply move on to the next question. The group will become comfortable with occasional pauses as the study progresses.

Your enthusiasm is infectious. Allow your interest in the topic to show. If you're fully engaged with the lesson's main points and questions, chances are your group will become engaged as well. Be careful not to ask questions like: "So, what did you get for number two?" Instead, rephrase the study's questions using your own words. Seek to create a tone of interesting and lively discussion.

People need encouragement. You can help make every person in the group feel valued by maintaining a steady stream of positive feedback. Respond to group members' comments, thank them for contributing, and let them know when they've said something that resonates with you. As you work to create an atmosphere of respectful appreciation for each other's thoughts, the group's participation and openness will increase.

Vulnerability must be fostered. Generally, people find it easier to discuss facts than feelings. Members of the group may feel tempted to give "right" answers instead of sharing their real thoughts about the issues raised in each study. When appropriate, talk about your struggles, questions, and concerns. Encourage others to share candidly as well. The group will learn best when both their minds and their hearts are affected.

The Holy Spirit will be your guide. Group discussions rarely go as expected. You pray, you plan, you prepare—and then the sessions inevitably take turns you never expected. Be flexible, and seek to discern God's leading through each lesson. Has a certain question sparked strong feelings or even disagreement? Perhaps God can use the opportunity to raise or clarify an issue. Has another question generated little response? Let it go. As you depend on God's guidance, you will find that he gives you wisdom to know how to best facilitate your group each week. No two sessions will be identical; don't try to make them so!

All's well that ends well. Conclude each lesson purposefully. Summarize the main points and raise application questions for the group to consider throughout the week ahead. Don't be afraid to challenge the group to live out what you've studied.

Remember, at the end of it all, it's not about you. It's about God. Serve him, point to him, rely on him—and then enjoy participating in what he chooses to do in your group.